15 MINUTES
of PEACE
WITH GOD

Emilie Barnes

HARVEST HOUSE™ PUBLISHERS

EUGENE, OREGON

Cover by Terry Dugan Design, Minneapolis, Minnesota

15 MINUTES OF PEACE WITH GOD

Copyright © 1997 by Harvest House Publishers
Eugene, Oregon 97402

Library of Congress Cataloging-in-Publication Data

Barnes, Emilie.
    15 minutes of peace with God / Emilie Barnes.
      p. cm.
    ISBN 0-7369-0726-2 (Softcover)
    ISBN 1-56507-625-7 (Hardcover)
    1. Meditations.   2. Devotional calendars.   I. Title.
    BV4811.B338   1997
    242'.2—dc20   96-34331
                                                            CIP

Printed in the United States of America

03 04 05 06 07 08 09 / BP / 12 11 10 9 8 7 6 5 4 3 2

Peace with God is a process of growing in the quiet places of our hearts by spending time alone with God.

I dedicate this book to the women who have passed through my life and placed in my heart a little bit of themselves. They have contributed to this book in ways that they know not.

Florence Littauer, Jackie Johnson, Jan King, Donna Otto, Jane Englund, Yoli Brogger, Joan Chambey, Barbara DeLorenzo, Ruth West, Sue Boydstun, Gertie Barnes, Judy Brixley, Susan Beck, Arlene Garret, my daughter Jenny, my daughter-in-love Maria, and many women across the country have all allowed me to be a part of their lives.

My prayer for you is found in John 14:27: "Peace I leave with you. My peace I give to you; not as the world gives do I give to you. Let not your heart be troubled, nor let it be fearful." Amen.

Peacefully,

Emilie

Emilie Barnes

15 Minutes of Peace with God

Traveling across America 20-plus times a year speaking to women has given me a real heart for their hurting hearts. "No time, no time!" they cry. "I have no time left for family, friends, housework, or meals—let alone time to spend a quiet moment with God."

I've written this devotional book for every busy woman who wants to get in touch with her Lord and her life. Each quiet time is designed to take 15 minutes or less. That's not a huge commitment, but it's an important one. You'll spend some time in God's Word, and you'll find helps and direction for your everyday life.

Another unique feature is that you don't have to start at the beginning and go chapter by chapter. You can skip around if you would like. In the top corner of each devotion you will see three boxes. Put a checkmark in one of the boxes each time you read that chapter. This way you can keep track of those devotions which you have read previously.

The 15-minute concept works! You just have to be willing to give it a try. Fifteen minutes a day for 21 days and you are on your way to devotions every day.

Allow God to hold your hand and lead you today to many quiet times with Him.

The only hope to the busy woman's cry is God Almighty Himself:

God the Father
God the Son
and
God the Holy Spirit.

I love you all. May the Lord touch each quiet time with Him.

—Emilie

Look to the Left, Look to the Right

Scripture Reading: Matthew 9:35-38

Key Verse: Matthew 9:36

He felt compassion for them, because they were distressed and downcast like sheep without a shepherd.

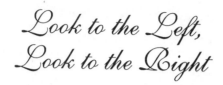

Each new day as I exit my front door and look to the left and to the right I find the world full of people who are distressed and downcast.

As I watch the morning news on my favorite TV channel I hear nothing but stories of people who are in distress and are downcast. As my Bob and I eat breakfast and go over the morning newspaper we are stunned by the articles in the paper:

- Pakistan blast kills 40
- Tens of thousands of Brazilians are reported toiling in bondage
- Boy six years old arrested for assaulting a month-old baby to near-death
- Gunman caught after killing 33 in Australia
- Apartment fire leaves 12 dead in Tijuana
- Bus bombed in protest of election; 15 dead
- Bus crash kills 31

- Trials set in killings of Brazilian street children
- $20 million frees abducted millionaire
- Zulu princess' body found at soccer field

After reading all of these depressing headlines, it's hard for us to finish eating breakfast. Yes, the world is full of people who are distressed and downcast.

In our passage for today we find Jesus teaching in all the cities and villages and proclaiming the good news of the gospel. As He looked at the multitudes He felt compassion for them. Yet in today's culture of violence we become desensitized to all the bad news we see, read, and hear. If it doesn't affect us and our friends we have a tendency to turn our heads and look the other way.

Maybe instead of looking to the left and to the right we should look *up toward God* and utter a prayer for all of those caught up in distress. We can't always do anything about people in foreign countries who face terrible problems, but we can look around and find people close to us in similar situations. Ask God to show you people you can help who face such dilemmas.

As Jesus showed compassion to those around Him, we too should show compassion. John Andrew Holmes is credited with saying, "There is no exercise better for the heart than reaching down and lifting people up."

This could mean a love basket of food, payment of a utility bill, a phone call of encouragement, babysitting while the person looks for a job, or a note saying you are praying for their situation.

Let's go beyond our comfort zone today and lift someone up who is down!

Father God, let me become aware of people
in my immediate surroundings who are distressed
and downcast. I'm not by nature a compassionate

person, but let me today take on one of Jesus' character traits: compassion. I thank You for what You are doing in my life regarding concern for others. Amen.

Taking Action

- 🐦 Make a love basket of food for a friend in need.
- 🐦 Write a note to a friend who has a particular need and tell her you are praying for her today.
- 🐦 Babysit for a friend who needs some free time to solve some of her problems.
- 🐦 Call someone in need and lift her up with good thoughts of encouragement.

Reading On

Matthew 28:19,20	Deuteronomy 30:3
1 John 3:17	Lamentations 3:22,23

Should we feel at times disheartened and discouraged, a simple movement of heart toward God will renew our power. Whatever He demands of us, He will give us at the moment the strength and the courage that we need.

—*Francois de La Mothe-Fenelon*

Where Can Wisdom Be Found?

Scripture Reading: Job 28:12-22

Key Verse: Job 28:12
Where can wisdom be found?

Not long ago my friend Florence Littauer wrote a book titled *Looking for Love in All the Wrong Places.* We are a culture which has a difficult time in reading the instruction manual. For some reason we want to invent the wheel by ourselves; we have trouble seeking the truth from the wise. We look for love in the wrong places, and we also seek wisdom in places where there is no wisdom. We talk to friends, read magazines, listen to talk shows, and attend seminars—all the wrong places.

The writer of the book of Job struggled with this same question of life. In Job 28:12 he asked, "Where can wisdom be found?" He too was perplexed with this question. All through chapter 28 he searched for the answer.

- Man doesn't know its value (verse 13a).

- It is not found in the land of the living (verse 13b).

- The inner earth says, "It's not in me" (verse 14a).

- The sea says, "It's not in me" (verse 14b).

- You can't buy it with gold or silver (verse 15).

- Precious stones don't have it (verse 16).

- It can't be equated with gold (verse 17).
- Pearls don't have it (verse 18).
- It is hidden from the eyes of all living creatures (verse 21a).
- Birds of the sky don't have it (verse 21b).
- Destruction and death say, "We have heard about it with our ears" (verse 22).
- God understands its way and He knows its place (verse 23).
- God looks to the ends of the earth and sees everything under heaven (verse 24).
- God saw wisdom and declared it (verse 27a).
- God established it and searched it out (verse 27b).

In verse 28 God told man, "Behold, the fear of the Lord, that is wisdom" (showing holy respect and reverence for God and shunning evil).

Job and his friends claimed wisdom of themselves, but wisdom is clearly an outgrowth of God and not merely something to be obtained. Although we can know and understand many things, we cannot attain to the level of Creator-wisdom. There will always be unanswered questions, for which only God the Creator will know the answer. Solomon knew that true wisdom is not found in human understanding but is from God alone (Proverbs 1:7; 9:10).

I challenge you to learn this basic truth of Scripture. If you want to know God's perspective, read your Bible daily; don't look in all the wrong places for your answers in life. Start with the manual that tells you step-by-step how to live life.

In John 10:10 we are told that Jesus came so we could have abundant lives. May our lives be richly blessed because of our faithfulness to the Scriptures. We don't have to wonder if God will trust us with His wisdom; the good news throughout Scripture is that the Lord gives wisdom liberally and without reproach to all of us who ask Him (James 1:5,6). If we approach the Lord in faith to show us what to do, what to say, and how to live, we can count on Him to give us His wisdom.

> *Father God, thank You for revealing to me where the true source of wisdom comes from. I truly want to show holy respect and reverence for You. As I read Your Word daily, I pray that Your truths will pop out to me and that I will continue to seek Your wisdom. May I never get to the point where I think I know everything about You. Thank You, Lord, for continuing to work in my life. Amen.*

Taking Action

- In what areas of your life are you seeking wisdom?
- Where can you go to find the answer?
- Is there a person you know who seems wise? If so, seek her out for godly counsel.
- Pray for the specifics of your need; let God know that you are seeking His guidance.

Reading On

Proverbs 1:7   James 1:5,6
Proverbs 9:10   Proverbs 8:18-21

Knowledge is horizontal.
Wisdom is vertical—
it comes down from above.

—*Billy Graham*

Stand By Your Convictions

Scripture Reading: Daniel 1:1-21

Key Verse: Daniel 1:8b

He sought permission from the commander of the officials that he might not defile himself.

A mother's joy would be complete if she heard that her son was making requests for healthful food. She would probably praise her son for actually wanting to eat nutritious foods and not just food from the fast-food restaurants.

In the book of Daniel we see a son who was raised by the teachings found in Leviticus 11. Daniel did not want to defile his body by eating foods that were unclean or had been offered to pagan idols before being put on the king's table. (Eating food offered to a pagan god was an indication of loyalty to that god.)

Notice the deep commitment of faith which enabled these young men to take the stands they took. They bore testimony to the faithfulness of mothers and fathers who taught them the central issues of obedience and faithfulness to biblical principles.

Because of this, Daniel was able to withstand the forces he faced in a hostile land. But since he was captured by the Babylonians and taken from his Israeli homeland, his mother may never have known the results of her early training while he was still in her home.

This value of teaching future generations has been impressed on me since I have two children and five grandchildren. We as mothers may never live to see how our children will respond as adults, but we must be faithful in raising our children to be responsible adults. I'm sure Daniel's mother prayed for him when he was young. She also continued to pray for him during the time of exile.

Whether or not she knew what Daniel had achieved, she had done the best job she could do as a mom: to raise a son who as an adult would follow the leading of the Lord.

As we look at our children we never know of their potential or what they will be as adults. But like Daniel's mother, we must continue as best as we know how to raise and prepare our children for God's calling.

> *Father God, at times I become so discouraged as a mom, because it seems like I'm the only one who cares. At times I sound like a squeaky wheel around my children and family. But You know that I want the very best for them. I want them to know of Your love for them, how to live a disciplined life, to be responsible for their actions, and how to have a healthful selection of foods. Even though I may not live to see them grown, I want You to know that my desire is to make them the children You would have them be. Thank You for putting that desire in my heart. Amen.*

Taking Action

- ❦ Do you have a plan to raise your children? What do you want them to become? How are they going to get there?

- ❦ Are you raising your children so they can think for themselves or are you still making all their decisions for them? Cut the cord early.

What areas of your life do you want to change so that your children are better equipped to face adulthood? Write them in your journal. What are you going to do to get there?

Reading On

Leviticus 11   Hebrews 11:23-28
Luke 2:41-52   Exodus 34:15

Discipline is demanded of the athlete to win a game. Discipline is required for the captain running his ship. Discipline is needed for the pianist to practice for the concert. Only in the matter of personal conduct is the need for discipline questioned. But if parents believe standards are necessary, then discipline certainly is needed to attain them.

—*Gladys Brooks*

Two Wisdoms

Scripture Reading: James 3:13-18

Key Verse: James 3:13

> Who among you is wise and understanding? Let him show by his good behavior his deeds in the gentleness of wisdom.

My husband, Bob, has an identical twin brother named Bill. When our children, Jennifer and Bradley, were very young and couldn't tell the men apart, they would address them as "two Daddies." When our grandchildren arrived, they also were confused when the two men were together. They would say "two PaPa's."

That's the way it is with wisdom. Both kinds are called wisdom, but they come from different sources, have different means, and most definitely have different ends. James talks about these two wisdoms in chapter 3:

- one which comes from above (verse 15).
- one which is earthly, natural, and demonic (verse 15).

The one that comes from above is—

- pure
  - peaceable
    - gentle
      - reasonable

- full of mercy
  - full of good fruits
    - unwavering (verse 17).

The second wisdom produces—

- bitter jealousy
  - selfish ambition
    - arrogance
      - lies against the truth (verse 17).

Notice the difference in the fruit that each produces:

- The first produces the fruit of righteousness and peace (verse 18).

- The second produces the fruit of disorder and every evil thing (verse 16).

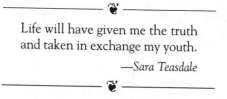

Life will have given me the truth
and taken in exchange my youth.

—*Sara Teasdale*

Wouldn't it be nice to have both wisdom and youth at the same time? Life, however, doesn't work that way.

Luci Swindoll states, "The good life is peace—knowing that I was considerate instead of crabby, that I stood by faithfully when all the chips were down for the other guy, that I sacrificially gave to a worthy cause, that I showed impartiality when I really wanted my preference, that I was real in the midst of phonies, that I was forgiving, that I had the courage to defer reward for something better down the road. Why couldn't I have learned this when I still had a young body?"[1]

Father God, I don't like my gray hair that reflects back to my eyes in the morning through the mirror. But my friends tell me I have wisdom in counseling and speaking. But why the gray hair? It doesn't seem fair that the two must go together. It seems like the world is drowning in knowledge, but we are starved for wisdom. Let me stand back and look at the real priorities of life. I don't want to chase rainbows that have no pot of gold at the end. Let me tell the difference. I want to say no to merely good things and save my yes for the very best. Amen.

Taking Action

- Which of the two wisdoms do you want to pursue?

- Meditate on your actions and see if they produce the right kind of fruit. If not, why not? What needs to be changed?

- Make a contract with a friend that she will hold you accountable to produce the fruit of peace and righteousness.

Reading On

Proverbs 4:5-7   Proverbs 9:10
1 Corinthians 2:6-13

There can be no wisdom
disjointed from goodness.

—*Richard C. Trench*

Who Fixed the Roof?

Scripture Reading: Luke 5:17-26

Key Verse: Luke 5:24b

He said to the paralytic, "I say to you, rise, and take up your stretcher and go home."

In our biblical study today we see several strands of truth. The passage opens with some friends of a crippled man who want to bring him to Jesus to be healed. When I was still a teenager my Bob invited me to his church to hear the gospel of Jesus proclaimed. Being raised in the Jewish faith and having just recently graduated from our synagogue's Hebrew school, I couldn't understand why Bob was so interested in having me come to church. In my heart I truly believed that I was perfect and was not a sinner.

Have you ever met anyone like that? As I look back, I see that Bob wanted me to be healed as a sinner and to become obedient to God's Word. Little did I know then that my future husband was willing to take me to the rooftop and lower me through the roof if that had been necessary. Bob truly cared for me, just as this sick man had friends who cared.

The sick man couldn't walk, so they carried him on his personal bed. Can you imagine how the people of the city stared as they watched a man being carried on his bed to see Jesus? As the group arrived at the house where Jesus was teaching they saw a large crowd of people and couldn't even get close to Jesus for the healing of their friend.

So one of the friends said, "Let's go over the crowd and take him up on the rooftop." Then they climbed up some outside stairs with the sick man on his bed. They reasoned that they had to take off some of the flat roof to lower the man and his bed inside the house near Jesus. I can just hear the dialogue that went on between the friends:

- This will be fun—like a party.
- We can't tear into a roof.
- The debris will fall down on top of Jesus.
- Who will fix the roof when we're finished?

Fortunately for the sick man, someone took control and started taking off a section of the roof. Then they tied ropes to the corners of the bed and let the man and his bed down through the hole in the roof.

You can imagine the amazement that Jesus and those in the crowd experienced as they saw a man and bed being lowered through the roof. Some could have thought:

- The nerve of them!
- Can't they take their turn?
- Gate crashers!
- Escort them out!
- Make them wait in line and take their turn like we did.

But Jesus looked at the man who had come down through the roof. Then He smiled and said, "Your sins are forgiven."

Some of the scribes and pharisees (Jewish leaders) were very upset. "Who does this Jesus think he is? Only God can forgive a man's sin!"

But Jesus replied, "You're right. Only God can forgive sins. I will show you that I can forgive sins." So He turned to the sick man and said, "Rise and take up your stretcher and go home."

At once the paralytic man rose up before them all and took up his bed and went home glorifying God. All the crowd watched in amazement and began to glorify God, for they truly had witnessed some remarkable things.

Fortunately, the friends hadn't spent time debating who would fix the roof. They just earnestly wanted to get their friend healed. Jesus also was open to a very unorthodox way in which the sick man was brought to Him, and the sick man was obedient to Jesus' command when He said, "Stand and walk."

The Bible clearly commands us to always obey the Lord (Acts 5:29; Daniel 7:27). In James 1:22 we are specifically required to hear His Word and do His will. We should be obedient to God because of our love for Him (1 John 2:3,4). These acts are to be a reflection of the inner reality that we truly love the Lord and are committed to His ways.

We know from raising children that obedience is not automatic. It must be taught and learned (Deuteronomy 6:7-9). We have security and peace when we are obedient to those in authority. (Maybe our disobedience is why we have so much unrest and violence today in our world, country, states, cities, families, and churches.)

I thank the Lord that my Bob cared for me so much that he took me to Jesus and I was healed. I'm also thankful that in childlike faith I said yes to the call of the gospel and made a conscious commitment to follow Jesus. It has been the most meaningful decision I have ever made in my life. Because of that submission to God and His Word, I am who I am today. Thank You, Jesus!

> *Father God, again I thank You that my Bob loved me so much that he wanted me to meet You and be healed. It was the event of my life. I can't imagine where I would be today without You. You have made all the difference. I'm glad to experience Your peace and restfulness. May I in turn be a caring friend who will reach out to someone who needs You. Amen.*

Taking Action

- Can you think of a friend who needs to be lowered through the roof?

- Invite that person to go with you to tea, a luncheon, shopping, a Bible study, a church event, etc. Even offer to come and get her.

- Minister to the needs (physical, social, emotional, and spiritual) of your friend.

Reading On

Acts 5:29	1 John 2:3,4
Daniel 7:27	Deuteronomy 6:7-9

The difference between perseverance and obstinacy is that one often comes from a strong will and the other from a strong won't.

—*Henry Ward Beecher*

Do You Love Me?

Scripture Reading: John 21:15-22

Key Verse: John 21:15a

Jesus said to Simon Peter, "Simon, son of John, do you love Me more than these?"

It seems as though we go through life wondering if our husbands, our children, and our friends love us. We feel insecure about the other people in our lives, and we're not sure where we stand. Even though we tell and show everyone we love them, they don't seem to catch the answer, because they're always reaching out to test our love for them.

Sometimes our children wear crazy clothes, put rings in their ears, color their hair in strange colors, and use foul language to see if we really love them. Our whole culture is continually testing us to see if we really love them.

In our passage today Jesus asks Peter three times (after His crucifixion and resurrection and Peter's recent denial of Him) whether Peter really loves Him.

I believe that these basic questions . . .

- Do you love Me? (verse 15)
- Do you love Me? (verse 16)
- Do you love Me? (verse 17) . . .

correspond to Peter's three denials of Jesus (John 13:38). Jesus in all His love for Peter wanted to give him a second chance to follow Him. He didn't want Peter to go all through life with the stigma of denying Jesus before His crucifixion. He wanted Peter to know that he was forgiven for his wrongdoings and that he could have a valuable ministry in spreading the gospel throughout the world.

But before Peter was able to confirm his love for Jesus, Jesus stated in verses 18 and 19 that the decision was going to cost him a price. In fact Peter and his wife were crucified upside down approximately 40 years later. After stating that there would be a price for following Him Jesus said, "Follow me," and Peter did.

> In repentance and rest is your salvation, in quietness and trust is your strength.
>
> —Isaiah 30:15 NIV

Yes, love has its price, not always to the extreme of Peter's, but a price of time, energy, commitment, money, and devotion. Selfish people take without giving back, but a true lover of people is always giving and giving and giving.

Is there someone in your life who is asking the very basic question "Do you love me?" What is your reply?

Father God, I know there are times when You ask me, "Do you love me?" I want to answer yes, and, like Peter, I want to follow You. Give me the courage to put my love into action. We can all answer yes, but it is only when we move into action that true love for You is demonstrated. Amen.

Taking Action

🐦 Write in your journal what actions of love you are going to do today for:

Jesus	Neighbor	Husband
Child	Friend	

❧ Do what you stated above. Be known as someone who does what she says she is going to do.

Reading On

1 John 4:7	1 Corinthians 13:1-8,13
1 John 4:10,11	John 14:21

When iron is rubbed against a magnet it becomes magnetic. Just so, love is caught, not taught. One heart burning with love sets another on fire. The church was built on love; it proves what love can do.

—*Frank C. Laubach*

Great Family Blessings

Scripture Reading: Ecclesiastes 4:8-12

Key Verse: Ecclesiastes 4:12
A cord of three strands is not quickly torn apart.

"I wish I had some good friends to help me in life!" cried lazy Dennis. "Good friends? Why, you have ten!" replied his master. "I'm sure I don't have half that many, and those I have are too poor to help me." "Count your fingers, my boy," said his master. Dennis looked down at his strong hands. "Count thumbs and all," added the master. "I have; there are ten," replied the lad. "Then never say you don't have ten good friends to help you on in life. Try what those true friends can do before you grumble and fret because you do not get help from others."

—Source unknown

Many times we look to others to help us out and complain when we don't receive the help we think we deserve. But help starts within ourselves, then moves outward. We need to take an inventory of all the skills and tools that God has so graciously given us at birth. We tend to take for granted those attributes of success which were given to us at the very beginning of our life. Our fingers and thumbs are such valuable tools for work. They truly are our dearest friends. In addition, King Solomon in all his wisdom told us that friends are great blessings to our family. He emphasized in Ecclesiastes chapter 4:

- Two are better than one because they have a good return for their labor (verse 9).

- Woe to the one who falls when there is not another to lift him up (verse 10).

- If two lie down together they keep warm (verse 11).

- Two can resist one who tries to overpower them (verse 12a).

- A cord of three strands is not quickly torn apart (verse 12b).

Are you working on relationships that build these kinds of blessings? Begin at home with your family members. Throughout Scripture we are told to be united with one another. Unity should be our goal as husband/wife, parent/child, child/sibling.

Begin to develop those traits that have eternal worth, not the temporal traits that live for such a short time.

In Ecclesiastes 4:8 Solomon asks one of the most basic questions of life: "For whom am I laboring and depriving myself of pleasure?" Is it all for vanity? Does it have redeeming value to you and your family? If not, do something about it.

> *Father God, in my heart and soul I want my family to be a blessing to me, and likewise I want to be a blessing to them. At times it seems to be in vain. Bring to mind those traits that are so important for friendships. I do want to be counted as a friend to those around me. Let me be a discerning person when it comes to doing my best for the people You have placed in my life. Let me major on major issues and minor on minor issues of life. Amen.*

Taking Action

❦ If you are married, discuss with your husband this question: "For whom am I laboring and depriving myself of pleasure?"

- ❦ What kind of friend are you? What qualities do you look for in a friend? Who would you consider your best friend? Why?

- ❦ Would you have wanted someone like yourself as a mother? Why or why not?

- ❦ Whom do you feel very comfortable around? Why?

Reading On

Proverbs 18:24   John 15:13
James 4:4   1 John 1:7

How little do my countrymen know what precious blessings they are in possession of, and which no other people on earth enjoy.

—*Thomas Jefferson*

□ □ □

Who Is Going to Bell the Cat?

Scripture Reading: Joshua 1:1-9

Key Verse: Joshua 1:9

Have I not commanded you? Be strong and courageous! Do not tremble or be dismayed, for the Lord your God is with you wherever you go.

———— ❧ ————

Once upon a time all the mice met together in council and discussed the best means of protecting themselves against the attacks of the cat. After several suggestions had been debated, a mouse of some standing and experience got up and said, "I think I have hit upon a plan which ensures our safety in the future, provided you approve it and carry it out. It is that we should fasten a bell around the neck of our enemy the cat, which will by its tinkling warn us of her approach."

This proposal was warmly applauded, and it had already been decided to adopt it when an old mouse finally got up on his feet and said, "I agree with you all that the plan before us is an admirable one, but I ask: Who is going to bell the cat?"

—Adapted from Aesop

Wouldn't it be wonderful if all we had to do in order to be brave is to talk about it? But true courage and bravery require *action*. Our society today hungers to find people with courage. We look for our heroes in sports, politics, movies, business, and church, but many of them fail the test. We hunger for the character trait of courage, but few people are able to deliver on it.

As parents we are continually tested by the decisions we must make. Are we able to stand alone and make hard decisions on what we as a family are going to do? It's hard to be in the minority as a friend, a neighbor, or a parent, to just say no. Unfortunately, the greatest pressure often comes from those we love the most!

In Joshua 24:15 the writer had a similar dilemma, but he stood tall and delivered this statement:

> If it is disagreeable in your sight to serve the Lord, choose for yourselves today whom you will serve: whether the gods which your fathers served which were beyond the River, or the gods of the Amorites in whose land you are living; but as for me and my house, we will serve the Lord.

Joshua was willing to stand up and be heard. He had the courage to bell the cat. Are you facing a similar difficulty in your life? If so, look to God to find the answer. He says He will never leave us or forsake us. That is a promise we can take to the bank.

We have some friends in Northern California who have made a "Valor Ribbon" for each of their two sons. When the parents are aware that the sons have taken some action that requires courage, bravery, or valor they recognize this fact by letting the boys wear their ribbon that evening at home. It might be for—

- not smoking, drinking, or taking drugs when someone offers them;
- not cheating on a test when the opportunity arises to do so;

- saying no to premarital sex;

- returning found money;

- assisting someone who is in need of help.

These parents recognize the importance of praising their sons' acts of courage.

Our reading today (Joshua 1:8,9) states:

- The law of Scripture shall not depart from your mouth.

- You shall meditate on it day and night.

- Be careful to do according to all that is written in it.

- This will make your way prosperous.

- You will have success.

- Be strong and courageous.

- Do not tremble or be dismayed.

- The Lord your God is with you wherever you go.

Let us not only talk the talk, but walk the walk, for God is always with us and we are never alone.

> *Father God, oh how I want to have courage enough to stand up and be counted in difficult situations. I really want to have the courage to bell the cat. Support me as I stand strong with my convictions. Don't let me waver as I stand tall. Let those around me gain strength from my strength which I receive from You. Let me not only believe the gospel but also behave the gospel. Amen.*

Taking Action

❦ In what areas of your life do you need to show courage? What are you going to do about the situation?

- You are offered a great buy on a beautiful jacket. You suspect it is stolen. Will you still buy it?

- The bank ATM gives you 60 dollars instead of the 20 dollars you asked for. What will you do?

- If you knew that a neighbor was abusing his wife and/or children, what would you do?

Reading On

Isaiah 41:10	Deuteronomy 33:27
Psalm 118:17	Philippians 4:13

Courage is doing what you're
afraid to do. There can be no
courage unless you're scared.

—*Eddie Rickenbacker*

Use Wisely What He Has Given You

Scripture Reading: Matthew 25:14-30

Key Verse: Matthew 25:29

> *To everyone who has shall more be given, and he shall have an abundance; but from the one who does not have, even what he does have shall be taken away.*

———— ❧ ————

God has given each of us specific talents—to some more than others, but to each of us *something*. What kind of stewards are we to become in using these talents? Some of us know from personal experience how a stuttering child can become an eloquent speaker and how a brilliant debater can become homeless when he uses his talent slothfully.

In today's passage we find Jesus telling His disciples that the kingdom of heaven is like a man who called his servants to delegate to them a portion of his property. To one servant he gave five gold coins, to another two coins, and to the third one coin. Each servant was given according to his ability.

The first man traded with his five coins and made five more. The man with two coins did likewise and made two more. But the one-coin man dug a hole in the ground and buried it.

After awhile the owner of the land came to settle the accounts with his three servants. The first servant brought with him the original five coins plus five additional ones. The master said, "Well done, good and faithful slave; you were faithful with a few things, I will put you in charge of many things" (verse 21).

The second man, who had been given just two coins, brought forth the original two plus the two he had made. The master likewise said, "Well done, good and faithful slave; you were faithful with a few things, I will put you in charge of many things; enter into the joy of your master" (verse 23).

The third servant came forward with the one gold coin and said, "Master, I knew you to be a hard man, reaping where you did not sow and gathering where you scattered no seed. And I was afraid and went away and hid your talent in the ground; see, you have what is yours" (verse 24,25).

But the master replied, "You wicked, lazy slave, you knew that I reap where I did not sow and gather where I scattered no seed. Then you ought to have put my money in the bank, and on my arrival I would have received my money back with interest. Therefore take away the talent from him and give it to the one who has the ten talents" (verses 26-28).

Then Jesus stated, "For to everyone who has shall more be given, and he shall have an abundance; but from the one who does not have, even what he does have shall be taken away" (verse 29).

This third man didn't mean any harm to the master, but he didn't understand the principles of stewardship and faithfulness. When we are faithful we are reliable: appearing on time, doing what we say we are going to do, finishing the job we started, and being there when we need to be there.

Everyday life operates on the laws of faith and trust. We assume that people are going to honor their word, stop at red lights, pay monthly mortgage payments, pay the utility bills, show up for an appointment, be faithful in marriage. Throughout Scripture God shows His attribute of being faithful.

We need women who will reach out with one or two or five talents and invest them wisely in their home, marriage, church, family, and community. We need women who will take the little they have and double it so that when we stand before Jesus He will say, "Well done, good and faithful servant; enter into the joy of my father's mansions." What a glorious day that will be!

Father God, I live in a world of comparisons, and I only see people who have five talents, while You seem to have neglected me by giving me only one. I feel, "how can I be as good as that person, since she has so much more than I do?" I pray that You would clearly show me how I can be faithful to the one talent that I have. Thank You, Lord, for all You have given to me. Amen.

Taking Action

- ❦ In your journal list three to five strengths that you have. Also list two or three weaknesses that you are aware of.

- ❦ Develop a plan of action to see how you will maximize your strengths. Likewise with your weaknesses, list actions that need to be taken to make these stronger.

- ❦ Ask a friend to help you with these ideas.

- ❦ Realize that you are special in the eyes of God.

Reading On

Psalm 127   Psalm 145:14
Psalm 139   Psalm 150

We make a living by what we get,
but we make a life by what
we give.

—*Winston E. Churchill*

Christians Are to Persevere

Scripture Reading: James 1:2-8

Key Verse: James 1:4

Let endurance have its perfect result, that you may be perfect and complete, lacking in nothing.

———— ❧ ————

A hare was one day making fun of a tortoise for being so slow on his feet. "Wait a bit," said the tortoise; "I'll run a race with you, and I'll wager that I win." "Oh, well," replied the hare, who was much amused at the idea, "Let's try it and see." They agreed that the fox should set a course for them and be the judge. When the time for the race came, both started off together, but the hare was soon so far ahead that he thought he might as well have a rest; so he lay down and fell fast asleep. The tortoise, meanwhile, kept plodding on, and in time he reached the goal. At last the hare woke up with a start and dashed on at his fastest, only to find that the tortoise had already won the race.

—Adapted from Aesop

Too many of us only see the start of the race and aren't around to see the end and find out who the real winners are. So much of life is painted with speed, flash, and sizzle that we get intimidated by everyone else's flash.

A few years ago our family went to Lake Tahoe to snow ski during the Christmas break. As I walked on the icy slopes of this beautiful resort my eyes were full of the best: the best of cars, of ski racks, of clothing, of beauty, of laughter. I couldn't believe my eyes—I had never seen so much sizzle in one place. Everyone was perfect!

So I said to myself, "No way am I going to compete with them." But after being coaxed into my group ski lesson I found that many of the "sizzle group" were also in my class and that they couldn't ski any better than I could!

The Scripture for today teaches that perseverance is *enduring with patience*. We will experience many trials in life that can discourage and defeat us. In the Bible, "perseverance" is a term used to describe Christians who faithfully endure and remain steadfast in the face of opposition, attack, and discouragement. When we persevere with patience, we exhibit our ability to endure without complaint and with calmness.

As believers we need to daily commit ourselves to godly living. Our daily commitments lead us to lasting discipline. I tell my ladies at our seminars, "It takes only 21 consecutive days to create a new habit."

Commitment and *discipline* are not words that the world is comfortable with. The nineties decade wants everything to feel good, and these words don't always feel good. They are words that demand denial of self and pain. "Feeling good" people don't like pain or testing; it makes them very uncomfortable, particularly when they don't trust the Tester.

Scripture is very clear when it teaches that we are to persevere—

- in prayer (Ephesians 6:18);
- in obedience (Revelation 14:12);
- in faith (Hebrews 12:1,2);

- in service (1 Corinthians 15:58);
- in self-control (2 Peter 1:5-7).

Scripture promises us certain blessings if we endure till the end:

- final deliverance (Matthew 24:13);
- rewarded faith (Hebrews 11:6);
- eternal inheritance (Revelation 21:7).

As we live out this life daily and are able to persevere in all its trials and temptations, we will be rewarded by the Lord with the fruit of His Spirit now and for all eternity (Galatians 5:22,23):

love	goodness
joy	faithfulness
peace	gentleness
patience	self-control
kindness	

> *Father God, please open my eyes to see that life is a laboratory that is developing Christian character in my life. Let me not get sidetracked by all the hares of life. I want to stay true to You during all the ups and downs of daily living. In life's difficulties I want to look heavenward to see what You are trying to teach me in these particular situations. May I always be faithful to Your Word. Amen.*

Taking Action

- ❧ In your journal list six blessings that God has given you.
- ❧ Also, jot down several struggles you are having in life. Beside each one list several things that God is trying to teach you through them.

Write down one desire of your heart. What are you and God going to do to make it a reality?

Reading On

Romans 5:3-5	2 Corinthians 4:14
Colossians 3:2	James 5:11

Great works are performed not
by strength, but by perseverance.

—*Samuel Johnson*

❑ ❑ ❑

A Yielding of the Heart

Scripture Reading: Luke 1:46-56

Key Verse: Luke 1:52

He has brought down rulers from their thrones, and has exalted those who were humble.

In the New Testament we find the word "humility" to mean a personal quality of dependence on God and respect for other people. It is not a natural human instinct but is a God-given virtue acquired through holy living.

While the mind of the natural man is selfish and proud, the essence of Jesus' mind is unselfish and loving toward others. Christ was our great example of a proper walk: pleasing to God.

Our hearts must be transformed by the Holy Spirit so that we can reflect God's love to others through the humble example of Jesus.

Corrie ten Boom, an unbelievable Dutch woman who survived the horror of World War II while in the confines of the German death camps, received a lot of praise for what she did during her confinement, and yet she remained unfazed by all the tributes. When asked how she managed to stay so humble among all these honors she humbly replied, "I accept every compliment as a flower and say thank you, and each evening I put them in a bunch and lay them at Jesus' feet, where the praise belongs."

Our world is full of men and women who are eager to take God's honor and heap it on their own heads. But God has a way of humbling us. From my own experience in life I know that I need to come before His throne with open arms and humbly bow before Him, seeking whatever He has for my life. We all need to learn this lesson of humility in life, because God has promised that if we don't humble ourselves, He will do it for us.

> To learn humility is to learn contentment in all circumstances. Humility is not in what we own or achieve, but in maintaining a teachable attitude, a willingness to bend to the will of the Father.
>
> —*Jan Silvious*

When Christ entered into the Greek world, they hated the quality of humility, but Jesus entered as a humble Savior. He became obedient to God's will, which led to His death on the cross. Throughout Jesus' walk on this earth He taught people to be humble before God and man.

In today's passage we see that God will exalt those who are humble. Humility comes from God and results in the praise of God.

Father God, You know how I want to lay down my bouquet of flowers at Your feet and give You all the praise. I know I am nothing without You. You have taken an ordinary woman and exalted her to a point at which I don't feel adequate. Thank You for fulfilling Your promise in me. Through my life may You be richly praised and lifted up. I am humbled that You can use me in life. Let me touch people so they know they have seen and felt Jesus. Amen.

Taking Action

- Ask God for a heart of humility.

- List in your journal three areas of pride that you have in your life. Beside each, state what you are going to do to turn pride into humility.

- Ask a friend to share with you those areas of your life where you need specific rearranging.

Reading On

James 4:10	Colossians 2:18
1 Peter 5:6	Romans 5:15

Unless you humble yourself before God in the dust, and confess before Him your iniquities and sins, the gate of heaven, which is open only for sinners saved by grace, must be shut against you forever.

—*Dwight L. Moody*

A Psalm of Thanks

Scripture Reading: 1 Chronicles 16:23-34

Key Verse: 1 Chronicles 16:34

> *O give thanks to the Lord, for He is good; for His lovingkindness is everlasting.*

I can't tell you how excited I get for fall to start—it's such an exciting time of the year! It also brings cooler temperatures in Riverside and we get to celebrate Thanksgiving Day. When I was a young Jewish girl we did not celebrate Christmas in our home, though Thanksgiving was acceptable. At home and in the neighborhood I could talk with my friends about this holiday.

However, for most of us it just meant that we had a day out of school (where we had reviewed all about the Pilgrims and Indians), we ate roasted turkey with all the trimmings, and of course we visited at one of our families' homes. This was a very festive occasion for a young girl. It wasn't until later in life that I really started to think about the blessings we receive when we are thankful.

Not until I met my Bob and his family did I begin to see all that I had and to mentally count these things with thanksgiving.

In our reading for today we see that we are to give thanks to the Lord, and not some other object. Why? because He is good and His love endures forever. Those are two things I was looking for in life:

- **GOODNESS**
- **EVERLASTING LOVE**

Our home certainly didn't reflect either of those. Instead, there was constant upheaval, with doors slamming and with waking at all hours of the night because of my father's drinking. I couldn't count on a love that was unconditional. I was loved when I performed, but it would be withdrawn for the slightest reason.

But Bob was different. He was a good person who seemed to have an everlasting ability to stand by his commitments. His family was so fun and easy to be around, one that modeled what I was so earnestly seeking. Here was a man that walked his talk.

I can still remember that first Thanksgiving feast in their home. The selection of foods was much different from ours, they prayed to tell God how much they appreciated all that they had (we always just dug in, with no time to thank God for what we had), and after the meal was over we went around the table expressing what we were thankful for. You mean to say that people actually thought about such things?

That evening as I got into bed I knew I was truly among a very special family, one much different from my past.

Later in life I discovered today's passage in 1 Chronicles:

> Sing to the Lord, all the earth;
>   proclaim his salvation day after day.
> Declare his glory among the nations,
>   his marvelous deeds among all peoples.
> For great is the Lord and most worthy of praise;
>   he is to be feared above all gods.
> For all the gods of the nations are idols,
>   but the Lord made the heavens.
> Splendor and majesty are before him;
>   strength and joy in his dwelling place.
> Ascribe to the Lord, O families of nations,
>   ascribe to the Lord glory and strength,
>   ascribe to the Lord the glory due his name.

Bring an offering and come before him;
>   worship the Lord in the splendor of his holiness.
Tremble before him, all the earth!
>   The world is firmly established; it cannot be
>   moved.
>   Let the heavens rejoice, let the earth be glad;
>   let them say among the nations, "The Lord
>   reigns!"
Let the sea resound, and all that is in it;
>   Let the fields be jubilant, and everything in
>   them!
Then the trees of the forest will sing,
>   they will sing for joy before the Lord,
>   for he comes to judge the earth.
Give thanks to the Lord, for he is good;
>   his love endures forever (1 Chronicles
>   16:23-34 NIV).

As I studied these verses, I began to pick out key action words and phrases that reflected how I should be worshiping God and how I was to model my new Christian walk. Some of these expressions were:

- Sing to the Lord.
  - Proclaim His salvation daily.
    - Share His marvelous deeds.
- God is worthy to be praised.
  - God is to be feared above all else.
    - God is not an idol but the Creator of the heavens.
      - God reflects splendor, majesty, strength, and joy.
- Ascribe to the Lord His glory.

- Bring an offering to Him.
  - The earth cannot be moved.
    - The heavens and earth are to rejoice and shout, "The Lord Reigns!"
- The sea, fields, and trees will sing joy unto God.
  - We are to give thanks unto the Lord.

Why? Because He is good, and His love endures forever! After reading this passage I realized I had been approaching God from the wrong direction. As my grandson, Chad, says, "We serve an awesome God."

I began to sing, to tell others about Him, and to praise God for His worthiness. I began tithing and I began to hear the sounds of nature as they sing praises to their Creator. Above all, I began to be scripturally thankful because of who God is.

Jesus was continually telling His disciples and those around Him that they could count on His continuing love. When you begin to have joy in the Lord, you get excited about seeing lives changed through the gospel. When you honestly begin serving and thanking God there will be real joy in your life.

Begin to count your blessings one by one. Meditate on all of them. Don't skim over them as you would the food section of your Thursday newspaper!

Father God, thank You for sending people in my life who have helped shape me into who I am today. Without them serving You in their daily lives, I would not have been able to see Your Word in daily application. As a mature lady looking back, I see that You have given me more than I would ever have wanted. Your abundance has been enormous. Thank You for keeping Your covenants to Your people. We are surely blessed. Amen.

Taking Action

- In your journal write down ten things for which you are thankful.

- Write down three things for which you aren't able to give thanks.

- With blind faith give these three items to God, knowing that in time He will reveal His purpose. (There are some events for which we will never know His purpose until we see Him face-to-face).

Reading On

Romans 8:28	Romans 10:17
Luke 17:5	Hebrews 11:1

Let all of us . . . give thanks to God and prayerful contemplation to those eternal truths and universal principles of Holy Scripture which have inspired such measure of true greatness as this nation has achieved.

—*Dwight D. Eisenhower,*
Thanksgiving Day Proclamation, 1956

❑ ❑ ❑

If I Had It All to Do Over

Scripture Reading: Luke 22:7-20

Key Verse: Luke 22:19b
This is My body which is given for you; do this in remembrance of Me.

———— ❦ ————

Someone asked me the other day if I had my life to live over, would I change anything?

My answer was no, but I thought about it and changed my mind.

If I had my life to do over again I would have waxed less and listened more.

Instead of wishing away nine months of pregnancy and complaining about the shadows over my feet, I'd have cherished every minute of it and realized that the wonderment growing inside me was to be my only chance in life to assist God in a miracle.

I would never have insisted that the car windows be rolled up on a summer day because my hair had just been teased and sprayed.

I would have invited friends over to dinner even if the carpet was stained and the sofa faded.

I would have eaten popcorn in the "good" living room and worried less about the dirt when you lit the fireplace.

I would have taken time to listen to my grandfather ramble about his youth.

I would have burned the pink candle sculptured like a rose before it melted while being stored.

I would have sat cross-legged on the lawn with my children and never worried about grass stains.[2]

Here is a woman looking back on life and remembering all the little phases and events we often overlook the first time around.

Each of us, regardless of what our ages are, look back with regret that we didn't take more time to _____. My Bob gets melancholy when we see our old photo slides of the children when they were young. He remembers when he could have if he would have. But we can't go back and re-capture lost opportunities. We need to take advantage of each day and live it to the fullest.

When we take communion at our church, the elements are placed on a table with these words carved on the side facing the congregation: "This Do in Remembrance of Me." The Scriptures state very clearly that we are to look back to the cross and remember what Christ did for us. At the communion table we are to—

- *Break bread:* "This is My body which is given for you; do this in remembrance of Me."
- *Drink from the cup:* "This cup which is poured out for you is the new covenant in My blood."

We are to remember what Christ Jesus did for us in history. Elisabeth Elliot states, "Ultimate hatred and ultimate love met on those two crosspieces of wood. Suffering and love were brought into harmony."

As we look back over our life, let's make sure that we have ac-cepted Jesus as He suffered for us and our sins on the cross and paid the price of His death because of His ultimate love for us. This un-selfish act has been the greatest event in human history. As we look back, may we clearly remember Jesus, the bread, and the cup of wine.

Father God, I remember back to when I was 16 years old; it seemed like just yesterday that I ac-cepted Jesus as my personal Savior. Through that very act You assured me that Jesus was my Messiah of the Old Testament. In one instant I had become a completed Jewish girl. As I remember back I have never regretted the decision I made one night on my knees beside my bed. You have been my strength and support over these years. Without You I fear what might have become of my life. You have been the difference between who I am and what I could have been. Reveal Your Son, Jesus Christ, to other women who are searching for meaning in their lives. Amen.

Taking Action

- Write in your journal your recollection of when you became a child of God: date, time, place, and situation.

- If you cannot write this down but would like to, select a pastor, a friend, a neighbor, or someone at work who is already a child of God and ask her to tell you about God's salvation through Jesus.

- When you are able to write this down as your own experience, do so. Also, write the date inside the front cover of your Bible. Then you will always have assurance when you doubt. You can look in your Bible and see written in your own handwriting the specific date when you first accepted Christ.

Reading On

Romans 3:23	Ephesians 2:8,9
Romans 6:23	Romans 10:9,10

He is no fool who gives
what he cannot keep to
gain what he cannot lose.

—*Jim Elliot*

Do Not Lose Heart

Scripture Reading: 2 Corinthians 4:7-18

Key Verse: 2 Corinthians 4:16,17

Therefore we do not lose heart . . . for momentary light affliction is producing for us an eternal weight of glory far beyond all comparison.

If you are having financial troubles, setbacks . . . it's not the end.

If you have been lied to and deceived . . . it's not the end.

If you have lost your job . . . it's not the end.

If you have lost your home . . . it's not the end.

If something has been stolen from you or if you have been robbed of your inheritance . . . it's not the end.

If you have a child who is ensnared in a sin, entangled in a web of wrong relationships, failing according to life's report card, or refusing to communicate with you . . . it's not the end.

If your mate has walked away, chosen someone else instead of you . . . it's not the end.

If you have just lost a loved one to death—sudden death, expected or unexpected—it's not the end. Even if your loved one committed suicide . . . it's not the end.

If you have behaved like an absolute fool and are mortified by what you did . . . it's not the end.

If you are incarcerated for a crime . . . it's not the end.

If you are losing your hearing or your sight . . . it's not the end.

If you are in the depths of depression, if you are battling

depression or a chemical imbalance that has thrown all your emotions and even your way of thinking out of kilter . . . it's not the end.

If you have learned that you have a terminal disease, a crippling disease, a wasting disease . . . it's not the end.

If you have stepped onto the threshold of death . . . it's not the end.

I can tell you all this with the utmost of confidence and know that what I am telling you is truth.

It may seem like the end . . .

you may wish it were the end . . .

but it is not the end because God is God and the end has not yet come.[3]

As I was reading this newsletter from Kay Arthur, thoughts of the past two years zipped through my mind. Often during this time I didn't want any more pain, heartache, or disappointments. I would ask God while walking the canal (my prayer closet), "God, aren't You finished yet? I thought yesterday's revelation was the end, but now You're telling me there is more!"

I so want to get through this situation of the present and move into something more positive in the future. Then God reveals to me that I get through the present day by remembering that it is not the end. I had been looking at the present condition as a negative, but He was telling me that I won't always be here (temporal), that the end (eternal) will be my final destination and that it will bring victory in all areas of my life.

The great women of the past were overcomers, and we too are overcomers. Each of us in our own way have realized victory in our walk with our Lord.

Whatever is born of God overcomes the world; and this is the victory that has overcome the world—our faith (1 John 5:4).

We too have a future and a hope because we belong to a covenant-keeping God. He never breaks His promises.

I am brought back to reality by reconfirming my faith in an almighty God and Father who reigns supreme over all.

I look upward and am reminded that I'm not to look at the things which are seen, but at the things not seen, for these have eternal value.

Father God, thank You again for reassuring me that this isn't the end, for the end will be an "eternal weight of glory" far beyond all comparisons. I know that what I'm thinking and feeling are only temporal, and though they really hurt, I trust You for the perfecting that's taking place in my life. I appreciate Your concern for me and my loved ones. Amen.

Taking Action

 In your journal list several of your temporary afflictions.

 Beside each one write, "This is producing an eternal weight of glory for me."

 Turn these over to the Lord in prayer and reconfirm your commitment to God, knowing that He reigns supreme over all.

Reading On

Jeremiah 29:11   1 John 5:4
1 John 2:17   Romans 8:28

God helps us to do what we can, and endure what we must, even in the darkest hours. But more, He wants to teach us that there are no rainbows without storm clouds and there are no diamonds without heavy pressure and enormous heat.

—*W.T. Purkiser*

□ □ □

Who Is the Greatest in the Kingdom of Heaven?

Scripture Reading: Matthew 18:1-6

Key Verse: Matthew 18:4
Whoever then humbles himself as this child, he is the greatest in the kingdom of heaven.

Jesus is saying that unbelievers need to humble themselves before the Lord as little children so they can gain salvation. In fact all of us need to humble ourselves until we become as a little child: exhibiting trust, openness, and eagerness to learn. These are the childlike qualities that constitute greatness.

Jesus used children as an illustration of the faith, trust, loyalty, and submission to God which are required in order to become part of His kingdom. The sharing of the gospel to children must be a priority for home and church. All believers have the assignment to model a godly life before the children in their presence and to love them and tell them about the Lord.

The gospel message is to be given to all, and a response is required by all who are old enough to know the difference between right and wrong (Matthew 28:19,20). Children are very capable of responding to God and can respond to Him in praise, worship, prayer, and thanksgiving.

In this passage Jesus does not tell children to become like adults but tells us adults to become like children. He also gives a very strong warning to those who might bring harm to these little ones. In Matthew 18:6 He states, "Whoever causes one of these little ones who believe in Me to stumble, it is better for him that a heavy millstone be hung around his neck, and that he be drowned in the depth of the sea."

That is a very serious statement of consequences, and therefore I want to do all within my power to take it seriously. We are to be teachers and edifiers with proper instruction for our children. In my latest book, *Fill My Cup, Lord*, I talk about a cup of prayer as found in Colossians 1:9-14. I want the reader to learn how to pray for their children. These little ones (or big ones— they still remain your children even though they are grown adults) need a hedge of prayer daily. A series of books that I find most helpful in praying the Scriptures for my children and grand-children is done by Lee Roberts and Thomas Nelson Publishers:

Praying God's Will for My Son
Praying God's Will for My Daughter[4]

These resources quote Scripture and let you insert the children's specific names so you can personalize your prayers. I have literally worn out my one book while praying for my daughter these last 2½ years. One of the side effects is that I see changes taking place in my own life. Oh, the Lord is certainly working in Jenny's life because of all my anointed prayers, but He is truly performing a miracle in my own life as well.

My friend Donna Otto has listed in her recent book *The Stay-at-Home Mom* ten ways in which a parent can pray for her children. She states: "Let's face it, without prayer anything else you do to influence your children for Jesus is feeble at best."

1. Pray that your children will fear the Lord and serve Him (Deuteronomy 6:13).

2. Pray that your children will know Christ as Savior early in life (Psalm 63:1).

3. Pray that your children will be caught when they're guilty (Psalm 119:71).

4. Pray that your children will desire the right kind of friends and be protected from the wrong kind (Proverbs 1:10,15).

5. Pray that your children will be kept from the wrong mate and saved for the right one[5] (2 Corinthians 6:14).

6. Pray that your children and their prospective mates will be kept pure until marriage[6] (1 Corinthians 6:18-20).

7. Pray that your children will be teachable and able to take correction (Proverbs 13:1).

8. Pray that your children will learn to submit totally to God and actively resist Satan in all circumstances: "Submit therefore to God" (James 4:7).

9. Pray that your children will be hedged in so they cannot find their way to wrong people or wrong places, and that wrong people cannot find their way to your children (Hosea 2:6,7).

10. Pray that your children will honor their parents so all will go well with them.[7]

The only assurance I have of access to my children's hearts is through prayer and the power of the Holy Spirit.

> *Father God, I have been challenged again today to be in earnest prayer for my children. As I survey the world and its changing attitudes toward children, I want to be a shining beacon supporting them in every way possible. You have inspired me to care for all of their other needs in life. Now You have placed on my heart a burden to pray and instruct them in the ways of the Lord. Amen.*

Taking Action

❧ Write the names of your children (grandchildren) in your prayer journal. Assign several pages for each child.

- Go through your recent photos and cut out a picture of each child. Glue it at the top of page 1 for each child.

- For each child write down at least one prayer request. Save room at the end of the request to note the date when you see an answer to that prayer. (In some cases be willing to allow weeks, months, and even years before an answer comes.)

- As time goes along, jot down other prayer requests for each child.

Reading On

Look up and read each verse of Scripture given earlier in the list of ten ideas on how to pray for your children.

The Reverend Moses Browne had 12 children. When someone remarked to him, "Sir, you have just as many children as Jacob," he replied, "Yes, and I have Jacob's God to provide for them."

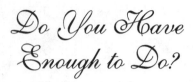

Do You Have Enough to Do?

Scripture Reading: 2 Thessalonians 3:6-15

Key Verse: 2 Thessalonians 3:10

> *Even when we were with you, we used to give you this order: if anyone will not work, neither let him eat.*

> The Camel's hump is an ugly hump
> > Which well you may see at the Zoo;
> But uglier yet is the hump we get
> > From having too little to do.
>
> Kiddies and grown-ups too-oo-oo,
> If we haven't enough to do-oo-oo,
> > We get the hump—
> > Cameelious hump—
> The hump that is black and blue!
>
> We climb out of bed with a frowzy head
> > And a snarly-yarly voice.
> We shiver and scowl and we grunt and we growl
> > At our bath and our boots and our toys;
>
> And there ought to be a corner for me
> (And I know there is one for you)
> > When we get the hump—
> > Cameelious hump—
> The hump that is black and blue!

The cure for this ill is not to sit still,
    Or frowst with a book by the fire;
But to take a large hoe and a shovel also,
    And dig till you gently perspire;

And then you will find that the sun and the wind,
And the Djinn of the Garden too,
    Have lifted the hump—
    The horrible hump—
The hump that is black and blue!

I get it as well as you-oo-oo—
If I haven't enough to do-oo-oo!
    We all get hump—
    Cameelious hump—
Kiddies and grown-ups too![8]

Life can be boring or exciting, depending on which you choose. Take time to look at your life's purpose and you can soon figure out how life is going. I've found that women who take the time to write out their "mission goals" and look to the future seem to have an excitement for life, but those who have never thought out what life is all about and only live for the moment seem to be bored with life.

My suggestion for living a happy life and not to grow a hump is to live life with a purpose. Give yourself away to a cause. Andrew Murray said it so well: "I have learned to place myself before God every day as a vessel to be filled with His Holy Spirit. He has given me the blessed assurance that He, as the everlasting God, has guaranteed His own work in me."

Some of us are called to labor by plowing or planting or harvesting. But each of us has a special calling to be used as a worker for God.

Often women ask me, "Do you get tired of what you're doing?" To be honest with them I say, "Yes, I do get tired of airports, airplanes, different time zones, the demands of people, and long lines waiting for an autograph, but seldom do I get tired of the ministry of my work." I get so excited when I can give a stressed mother peace, assurance, self-confidence, and a renewed walk with our Lord.

May you grasp the excitement of living life with a purpose. Do what you like to do before the Lord and do it with all the energy and creativity you have, regardless of the social ranking or prestige of the calling.

David the psalmist wrote in Psalm 37:4,5, "Delight yourself in the Lord, and He will give you the desires of your heart. Commit your way to the Lord; trust also in Him, and he will do it."

Two words stand out to me in this passage: *Delight* and *commit*. These are both action words that require us to do thinking and planning. Remember to live life with a purpose, not by accident. You can take control of your own life, so don't wait for others to determine your fate in life. With God's help you can find complete enjoyment and can arise each morning with a song in your heart and a bounce in your walk. In fact, people will stand back and ask you, "What's come over you? There's something different about you!"

> *Father God, You know how exciting life is for me.*
> *I have so many wonderful things to accomplish. I truly*
> *do have a delight for You and I want to continue com-*
> *mitting my ways to You. I can't comprehend people*
> *who think life is boring. Give me the strength and health*
> *to encourage women to be all that You have for them.*
> *Let them want to be women after God's design. Amen.*

Taking Action

❦ In your journal write a mission statement expressing what you want out of life. Find a verse of Scripture that supports this statement.

❦ Write down three desires that you have.

❦ What are you going to do to make these desires

a reality?

 Commit all of these to the Lord.

 Pray for the desires of your heart.

Reading On

Psalm 8:3	Romans 11:6
Psalm 111:3	James 1:25

> The law of nature is that a certain quantity of work is necessary to produce a certain quantity of good of any kind whatever. If you want knowledge, you must toil for it; if food, you must toil for it; and if pleasure, you must toil for it."
>
> *—Ruskin*

□ □ □

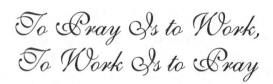

To Pray Is to Work, To Work Is to Pray

Scripture Reading: Proverbs 31:10-31

Key Verse: Proverbs 31:31

> *Give her the product of her hands, and let her works praise her in the gates.*

For some reason we think that women going to work started during World War II, when women had to fill the gap while the men were away defending our country. But today's Scripture reading goes back to about 800 years B.C. Long before we even thought of women being in the labor force, this capable woman was an energetic, hard worker who labored far into the night.

We see her virtues by looking at the following verses in Proverbs 31:

- 13: She looks for wool and flax. She works with her hands in delight.

- 14: She is like a merchant ship. She brings her food from afar.

- 15: She rises before sunup. She feeds her household. She gives to her maidens.

- 16: She considers real estate. She has her own money. She plants vineyards.

- 17: She works out and is in good physical shape.

- 18: She analyzes her profits. She plans ahead. She works into the night

- 19,20: She gives to those in need.

- 21: She sews her household's garments.

- 24: She sews to sell for a profit.

- 25-27: She radiates good business practices.

- 28,29: She attracts compliments from her family.

- 31: She exudes excellence from her work and is praised in her neighborhood.

This woman knew all about work even though she didn't have an MBA from Harvard or Stanford. She was a woman who feared (respected) God, and because of her noble efforts in the workplace she was praised.

In today's work climate we find that Monday is the most difficult day of the week—the most absenteeism, the most accidents, the most illnesses. Many of today's workers focus on Fridays—the getaway days. In fact, a popular restaurant is named TGI Friday (Thank God It's Friday). If you go into this restaurant to eat, you sense a party atmosphere. It's a place to forget all your cares. Let's have a party!

This attitude has a lot to say about modern man's approach to work. It's a far cry from the day when the adage was "To pray is to work, to work is to pray." In those days work was a reflection of worship to God. When we worked we worked to the Lord, not the pleasing of man. That's when the artisan was a creator of excellence in art, music, literature, and the professions. Martin Luther once said that a man can milk cows to the glory of God. It is our own attitude toward work that reflects the joy of the Lord.

Oh, if we could recapture this concept of work! We would take the drudgeries of everyday life and give them to God. If we took the routines surrounding our work and began to pray about them, I believe our whole attitude would change for ourselves and those in our family. No longer would we wait for the whistle to blow on Friday so we could let the real life begin. For us every day would be a Friday.

In Genesis we read that in the beginning God *created*. He believed in the honor of work. It was a godly activity. It was not cursed, as it is today. God worked for six days and then rested. How is your rest period? Do you get any?

Jesus, a carpenter, was a worker making goods out of wood. The Scriptures teach that if we aren't willing to work we shouldn't expect to eat.

How do we learn that to pray is to work, and to work is to pray?

- Each morning when we wake up we thank God for a new day and all that is in it.

- We offer to God in worship all of our energies, creativity, time, and skills.

- We recognize that work done in an attitude of prayer brings excellence, which in turn bears testimony to God.

- We realize that we are obedient to God when we provide for our family and their needs.

- We model to our children that work is good, so that they see us give worship to God for the work He has given us.

> *Father God, at times when I face the drudgeries of all that I have to do, when I wipe the sweat from my brow and my back aches from the weight of lifting, I forget that how I do my job is a reflection upon my worship to You. I truly want to wake up each morning with a song in my heart and an eagerness to start a new day. In the evening before I fall asleep*

I want to praise You for another day's work. Let me be in continuous prayer while at work. Let me work for You and forget about the praises of man. Amen.

Taking Action

- Assign prayer to your work.

- Thank God for the skills He has given you to perform worship to Him.

- Does your work reflect excellence? If not, what can you do to change this? Note it in your journal.

- Are you remembering to rest one day a week?

Reading On

Ecclesiastes 2:11   Titus 3:8
Matthew 5:16   Psalm 8:3

It is our best work that He wants, not the dregs of our exhaustion. I think He must prefer quality to quantity.

—George MacDonald

□ □ □

Home Rules

Scripture Reading: Deuteronomy 6:1-9

Key Verse: Deuteronomy 6:7a
You shall teach them diligently to your sons.

———— ❧ ————

Home is the one place in all this world where hearts are sure of each other. It is the place of confidence. It is the place where we tear off that mask of guarded and suspicious coldness which the world forces us to wear in self-defense, and where we pour out the unreserved communications of full and confiding hearts. It is the spot where expressions of tenderness gush out without any sensation of awkwardness and without any dread of ridicule.[9]

In our Scripture passage today God outlines the responsibility that we have as parents to teach our children at home and in other venues that are appropriate. So important were the commands of the Lord that Moses directed us to do everything possible to remember these commands and to incorporate them into everyday life.

The spiritual education of the children was the responsibility of the parent. The teaching would take place daily through the example of the parents as well as through the repetition of the law. The importance of this command is seen by the extent to which parents were to go in order to teach their children. This was more than simply teaching the facts of the law; it was to be the demonstration of a lifestyle woven into the tapestry (see verses 8,9) of everyday life. Creativity is essential in teaching the precepts of God while we are involved in mundane chores of the household.

CHARACTER AND CONDUCT

Conduct is what we do; character is what we are. Conduct is the outward life; character is the life unseen, hidden within, yet evidenced by that which is seen. Conduct is external, seen from without; character is internal—operating within. . . . Character is the state of the heart, conduct is its outward expression. Character is the root of the tree, conduct, the fruit it bears.

—*E.M. Bounds*

Today that becomes our biggest task—to teach Christian values and responsibilities in a creative fashion. How can we compete with TV sound bites, Disney mindset, computers, and laser printers? We live in an age of fast-paced technology that throws fast, colorful, and short concentration bites of information to all of us, including our children.

It takes creative parenting to teach our young ones biblical principles. Often our children pick up on our walk better than on our talk. They have great discernment in observing how Mom and Dad (and other adults) live out these principles.

In verse 7 we find that teaching and learning doesn't always take place in a formal, rigid classroom setting. We are to talk of these principles when we sit in our house, when we walk by the way, when we lie down, and when we rise.

Twenty-four hours a day we can integrate biblical truths in everyday settings.

Ann Landers printed a set of Home Rules from a lady in California:

> If you sleep on it—
>   make it up.
>
> If you wear it—
>   hang it up.
>
> If you drop it—
>   pick it up.
>
> If you eat out of it—
>   put it in the sink.
>
> If you spill it—
>   wipe it up.
>
> If you empty it —
>   fill it up.
>
> If it rings —
>   answer it.
>
> If it howls —
>   feed it.
>
> If it cries —
>   love it.[10]

If your children understood these nine simple rules when they started kindergarten, the teacher would sing praises to your name, for these form the basic foundation for citizenship. It is amazing how many adults can't demonstrate these simple, basic manifestations of responsibility.

> *Father God, being a godly parent is not easy. Sometimes I just want to go back to the simple life without having to face the awesomeness of raising children. I get so tired and weary of being the one to transmit virtue values to the next generation. Restore in my soul*

the desire to keep on keeping on. There are some days when I think it's impossible to continue with what I feel is an endless task of teaching my children. Please reassure my faith in what I've set out to do—to be obedient to Your commands. Amen.

Taking Action

- Take a three-by-five card and print one of the home rules on it. Take it to the dinner table and discuss how you as a family can incorporate the rule into this week's schedule.

- Do the same for each of the nine rules. After the ninth week, go back and review how you did.

- Bring back for another week those rules that need more work done on them.

Reading On

Deuteronomy 11:18-20   Ephesians 6:4
Proverbs 22:6   2 Timothy 3:15

The Bible doesn't say very much about homes; it says a great deal about the things that make them. It speaks about life and love and joy and peace and rest. If we get a house and put these into it, we shall have secured a home.

—*John Henry Jowett*

Make Breakfast and Lunch for Jesus

Scripture Reading: Genesis 2:8-25

Key Verse: Genesis 2:18

> *The Lord God said, "It is not good for the man to be alone; I will make him a helper suitable for him."*

———— ❧ ————

Several years ago I was teaching a women's Bible study in our home, and one Friday morning we had a lesson on the creation of women and their role in marriage. When we came upon this passage there was a lot of discussion about the role distinction between men and women and what God intended when He created both.

We eventually got around to discussing how we could be helpers to our husbands, and of course this sparked a lot of controversy, especially when I casually mentioned that I got up early in the morning and prepared Bob's breakfast and his lunch for work. One of the young women was having difficulty accepting this concept and said, "I could never do that for my husband!" In a kind fashion I asked her why, and her reply was that he wouldn't appreciate it, and besides, she liked to sleep later in the morning.

In a split instant a brilliant thought came to my mind. I looked this lady in the eye and asked, "Jane, would you be willing to get up and make Jesus breakfast and lunch?"

Without a moment's hesitation she replied, "Yes." So I instructed her, "Then don't make breakfast and lunch for Bill, but make them for Jesus." "I can do that without any problems," responded Jane.

To this day both Jane and Bill credit this idea as the most instrumental turning point in restoring their love for each other, even though for some years Bill wasn't aware that Jane was making breakfast and lunch for Jesus. When Jane saw Bill's response toward this love gift, she soon started making breakfast not just for Jesus but for her husband as well.

Here was a woman who was willing to try something new in life: She trusted God to enable her to be a helper to her husband.

LORD OF ALL POTS
AND PANS

Lord of all pots and pans and things,
Since I've no time to be
A saint by doing lovely things
Or watching late with Thee,
Or dreaming in the dawnlight
Or storming heaven's gates,
Make me a saint by getting meals
And washing up the plates.

Thou who didst love to give men food
In room or by the sea,
Accept this service that I do—
I do it unto Thee.

—*Author Unknown*

God in His marvelous plan knew what He was doing when He created marriage. Marriage was perfect in its establishment: one man and one woman in a lifetime commitment.

From the very beginning (Genesis 2:18) God never intended for man to be alone. Woman was taken out of man, then presented to him in order to complete him (Genesis 2:22,23). Ladies, do you look upon your purpose in life as a completion for your husband? If you do, then you and your husband will receive blessings that come from this mindset. As I look around I see many women who don't realize that their husbands aren't functioning properly because their wives aren't willing to be their helper.

In Genesis 2:24 we see that we need to lay aside all our old loyalties and lifestyles of separate goals and plans and instead be joined together as one. This bond produces a much stronger result than either individual had produced separately (Ecclesiastes 4:9-12).

No human relationship is to be stronger than the bond between husband and wife. Marriage is a vow made to God not only to love but also to be faithful and to endure in this lifelong togetherness.

Even in the church we have lost the miracle meaning of marriages. We have become conformed to the world (Romans 12:2) and aren't willing to be transformed by the renewing of our minds.

The miracles of marriage are:

- We are joined together socially.
- We become one flesh biologically.
- We reflect the relationship between God and His bride (the church) spiritually.

Oneness is the strength of any marriage. Women, you and I play a tremendous part in marriage when we learn and exhibit the helper role that God has intended us to have. Can you honestly state that your husband is complete because you are his wife? If not, you might want to make Jesus breakfast and lunch. Take a risk and be all that God wants you to be!

Father God, I thank You for letting me learn

many years ago about my role as a helper for my husband. By Your grace I don't have to feel inferior or that I'm going to be taken advantage of. Over the years I know that Your plan works—I have experienced it in my own life and have borne witness to it in the lives of many other women. I know that for some women this is all a new idea to them, but may they be willing to serve Jesus by making His breakfast and lunch. Amen.

Taking Action

- In your journal list five things you do that make you feel like you are completing your husband.

- List three areas that you are having difficulty with. What can you do to help yourself in these areas?

- Ask a friend to support you in prayer concerning what needs to be done.

- Have her check back with you at least every two weeks to hold you accountable in these areas.

- Pray specifically that God will help you strengthen these areas.

Reading On

I Corinthians 13:4-8   Hebrews 12:5-11
Proverbs 31   Ephesians 5:23-27

God is our refuge and strength,
a very present help in trouble.
—*Psalm 46:1*

❑ ❑ ❑

Complement, Not Compete

Scripture Reading: Ecclesiastes 4:1-12

Key Verse: Ecclesiastes 4:9,10

> *Two are better than one because they have a good return for their labor. For if either of them falls, the one will lift up his companion. But woe to the one who falls when there is not another to lift him up.*

A couple of years ago my Bob and I were speaking at the Southern California Women's Retreat. I was introducing my new book, *The Spirit of Loveliness*, and he was speaking to the 700 ladies on his new offering, *Your Husband, Your Friend*.

As Bob was finishing up his presentation he had a few minutes before closing, so he opened the floor for questions. The first question was from a middle-aged woman who asked: "Bob, aren't you threatened as a man when your wife has written so many books and is asked to speak all over the country?" With a slight pause Bob replied, "No, because Emilie and I aren't in competition, but we complement each other." Many of the women applauded the response.

When word got back to me about Bob's answer, tears filled my eyes, because I realized the growth that had taken place in my Bob's life.

For 28 years of our married life I had always been "Bob's

wife" because he was the breadwinner. He brought home the checks with his name on them. But when Bob decided to help me in our growing ministry, he all of a sudden became "Emilie's husband," since checks were made out in my name and not his.

For a man this is a most difficult situation, since a man's work is his worth. I'm sure that the all-time low for Bob came when a lady approached him at one of our seminars and wanted to know if he was Mr. Emilie Barnes!

No matter how we may try to do otherwise, we live in a competitive world that rates people by performance. So for my Bob to state that we weren't in competition with each other but that we complemented each other showed remarkable growth in his life.

I can truly say that he lives out that principle in our lives. I continually get told what a valuable asset he is to me and our ministry. I could not do what I'm doing without his input, creativity, energy, love, and support. Where I am weak, he is strong. He encourages me to use the strengths that God has given me and he fills in the gap where he is gifted.

> Your husband will never truly
> be yours until you have first
> given him back to God. He is
> yours only when you are willing
> to let him go wherever God
> calls him and do what God
> wants him to do.
>
> —*Lila Trotman*

The longer I live the more I realize that two are better than one. Our passage for today reinforces this concept, and I can tell you how true it becomes in real life—not only as we get older, but through all the trials and testings of our youth.

As we travel in ministry and in pleasure, we observe other couples who have decided to complement, not compete. What a soothing effect this has in all our relationships! The Scriptures are full of verses that emphasize unity and oneness.

If I had one recommendation for couples who want strong marriages, I would stress this concept of oneness. Women, I challenge you to examine your relationship with your mate (if you are married) and see whether you have a marriage built on oneness or are just going your separate way. If your marriage is one of separation, I encourage you to begin anew and set out to become one. If you reflect oneness, I thank the Lord for that. Continue to model before others what God has given you as a couple. The world is hungry to see proper modeling of His Word.

Suzanne Wesley once stated that there are two things you do with the gospel:

- You believe it.
- You live it.

How do we grow into oneness? We begin to:

- Trust our mate.
- Understand our mate.
- Verbally praise our mate.
- Be mutually accountable to each other.
- Love each other just as Christ loved us.
- Give and accept forgiveness when necessary.

> *Father God, how I am encouraged to realize that my husband truly wants us to be one. I'm thankful that You have given me such a man. However, I realize that this isn't the case in all homes. May You touch the woman who wants this to be true and give her clear direction to work toward that goal. May she realize the blessings of such unity. Amen.*

Taking Action

- In your journal write down your desire to have a marriage that stresses oneness. What are you going to do to make it happen?

- Pray for your mate that he will grasp the same desire.

- Share with your mate how God has challenged you in this direction.

- Ask your husband to support and encourage you in this decision.

Reading On

Genesis 2:23-25   1 Corinthians 12:12,13
Philippians 2:1-4   1 Corinthians 12:26,27

A selfish person works in competition with others. He misses the rewards of cooperation.

What Would Jesus Do?

Scripture Reading: 2 Timothy 3:10-17

Key Verse: 2 Timothy 3:15

> *From childhood you have known the sacred writings which are able to give you the wisdom that leads to salvation through faith which is in Christ Jesus.*

———— ❦ ————

One evening while sitting around the meal table with our grandchildren, we had a discussion of what to do when Mom and Dad were not around to tell them right from wrong. We love those kinds of discussions because then we can teach moral values without preaching to the grandchildren.

For some reason the thought came to my mind "WWJD?" They all looked funny at me and asked, "What's WWJD?" Without a moment of hesitation I replied, "What would Jesus do?" Christine, our oldest grandchild, replied, "That's good, Grammy, I like that." She went on to express how she often has to decide when she is with friends, "Should I do that or should I not?" Then she added, "WWJD will help me make wise choices." Even as adults, we could ask ourselves when these situations come up, "WWJD?"

Now when something comes up when the grandchildren ask a "What should I do?" question, we just say, "WWJD." Enough has been said. They know just what we mean.

Today's verses teach that from childhood you have known God's Word, which is able to give you wisdom. Who is responsible for this dissemination—the schools, the government, the church? No, the primary responsibility falls upon us as *parents* to teach our children the Scriptures. In Deuteronomy 6:6-9 Moses tells us as parents to:

- teach Scripture diligently to our children;

- talk to our children about Scripture when we sit in our home, when we walk by the way, when we lie down, and when we rise up;

- bind Scripture as a sign on our hands and as frontals on our foreheads (see Exodus 13:9);

- write Scripture on the doorposts of our house and on our gates.

This sounds like serious stuff to me. Children can't achieve good moral values while watching and reading some of the material offered in our society today.

If our children are to stand a chance to survive and be able to escape all the evils around them, they must have spiritual ammunition to ward off the enemy. We are no longer playing for fun. Life must be lived with a purpose, and we as parents are to guide our children into wise choices through proper instruction in the home. This can't be left to the church, the Sunday school teacher, the Awana leader, or the Boy Scout/Girl Scout leaders. Nowhere in Scripture are those mentioned. Yes, they can help, but we as parents are given the commands to teach our children at an early age.

At the end of his life Joshua made a challenging statement: "You may serve whatever god you want, but as for me and my house, we will serve the Lord." Yes, it begins with Dad, then Mom, and then the children. We must choose which god we will serve. We have to stand up and be counted if we are going to live life with a purpose. The road is narrow, and it is the road less traveled.

If we are going to tell our children "WWJD?" they need to know Jesus well enough to have a storehouse of information about who He was and is today.

Father God, today You have made me realize what an awesome job it is to be a parent. As I see my children and grandchildren struggle to keep their heads above water, I want them to have instant maturity. May You come alongside them and put a protective fence around them. Life is such a struggle even when we know Your Word. I can't imagine what it is like without having Your Scripture in my mind. Thank You for being there when I need You. Amen.

Taking Action

- ❦ Go to your pastor or a trusted friend for a recommendation on good study materials.

- ❦ Set aside time daily to meet with your children to read and discuss God's Word. You might start with the book of John.

- ❦ Place a chalkboard somewhere in your home and use it to write down those specific verses that have been meaningful to you and your family. Change the verses at least once a week.

- ❦ Each week use three-by-five cards to jot down certain verses of the Bible for you and your children to memorize. Hold each other accountable. Work on these daily.

Reading On

Ephesians 6:4   Joshua 24:15
Deuteronomy 6:6-9   Exodus 20:1-17

---··---

The study of God's Word, for the purpose of discovering God's will, is the secret discipline which has formed the greatest characters.

—*James W. Alexander*

---··---

We Have to Burn Our Ships

Scripture Reading: Matthew 19:3-9

Key Verse: Matthew 19:6b
What therefore God has joined together, let no man separate.

———— ❧ ————

Hernando Cortés had a plan.

He wanted to lead an expedition into Mexico to capture its vast treasures. When he told the Spanish governor his strategy, the governor got so excited that he gave him eleven ships and seven hundred men. Little did the governor know that Cortés had failed to tell him the entire plan.

After months of travel, the eleven ships landed in Veracruz in the spring of 1519. As soon as the men unloaded the ships, Cortés instituted the rest of his plan: He burned the ships.

That's what you call commitment. That's what you call no turning back. That's what you call burning your bridges. Cortés didn't have any bridges, so he burned the ships.

By burning the ships, Cortés eliminated the options. He didn't know what he would encounter on his expeditions to the interior. He didn't know the strength of the people he would be fighting. But he did know this: There were now no escape routes for his men. If the fighting got too fierce or the expedition got too exhausting, there would be no talk of going back to Veracruz and sailing home. In one fell swoop he had not only eliminated their options but had created an intensely powerful motivation to succeed. Like it or not, they were now committed.[11]

That's the kind of fervor we must have in our own marriages—both husband and wife. There are no options to be considered. When our children see that Mom and Dad love each other there is a settling effect over the family.

Burning the ships expresses that there is no turning back, no matter what. We are committed to our marriage. I realize that in today's culture there are situations that make this very difficult. Sometimes we may not have a vote, but in most cases we are able to stand and defend our marriage.

Commitment means that no matter what comes into the future we are going to stick it out. We are obligated to follow through on the words of our marriage vows.

The nineties is the "Don't I have a right to feel good decade?" Everyone wants to feel good. If it doesn't feel good, don't do it. Change until it feels good again. Go for awhile with whatever you're doing. When that stops feeling good, change until it feels good again.

There are times in a marriage when the bells and whistles stop making joyful noises. But just because we don't *feel* like we're married doesn't mean we *aren't* married. In today's key verse Jesus commands that if we have been joined together by God, let no one separate us. These are strong words. In essence Jesus is saying, "Burn the ships."

We live in a day when commitment means little. Every day we see a lack of it in politics, sports, business, and marriage. Everyone wants to renegotiate their contracts. In the old days a shake of the hand between two people was as good as a signed contract. But today even signed contracts mean very little. Commitment is a cheap word. We only honor commitment when it is convenient.

The sixties should have taught us that when we are doing our own thing we are being selfish. Selfishness is the number one crime that ultimately destroys a relationship.

When Bob and I were married, our vows to each other stated that we were to be committed in sickness and in health, for richer or for poorer, for better or for worse, until death would part us. These are strong words, but they mean very little if taken lightly. For the words to be meaningful, the ships must be burned in the harbor.

How can you love your mate? By daily *choosing* to love him. Every day, not just when it's convenient. Love is a choice, not a feeling. We have been misled by the "feeling" advocates. We need to get back to the Scriptures and see what God says about commitment and marriage.

We often hear a person stating, "But I just don't have chemistry for him anymore." Our loving pastor states that the only "C" of marriage mentioned in the Bible is *commitment*.

Are you willing to burn your ships in the harbor?

> *Father God, as I read today's words of instruction from Your Word, I'm challenged to examine my own life to see if I've held out on burning the last few ships I've hidden for escape. I need Your help to hold me up when I feel so weak. I need more help in trusting my mate in all of our affairs. Give me today enough faith to destroy those few remaining ships. Today I promise to burn all the ships that remain. Amen.*

Taking Action

❧ Burn any remaining ships that you have in the harbor.

❧ In your journal write the names of these ships you have burned.

- Share with your mate how much you love him and how much you appreciate all he does to make the family united.

- Send your husband a love note at his work. Tell him you can't wait until he gets home this evening.

- If you can do so comfortably, share with him how you've made a new commitment to the success of your marriage.

Reading On

Genesis 1:27	Deuteronomy 24:5
Genesis 2:23,24	Proverbs 31:23

A happy marriage is the union
of two good forgivers.

— *Robert Quillen*

Be a Living Presence

Scripture Reading: Psalm 127:1-5

Key Verse: Psalm 127:3

*Behold, children are a gift of the Lord; the fruit of womb
is a reward.*

———— ❦ ————

The young mother asked her guide about the path of life.

"Is the way long?" she inquired.

And her guide replied: "Yes. And the way is hard. And you will be old before you reach the end of it. But the end will be better than the beginning."

But the young mother was happy, and she would not believe that anything could be better than these years. So she played with her children, and gathered flowers for them along the way, and basked with them in the clear streams; and the sun shone on them and life was good, and the young mother said, "Nothing will ever be lovelier than this."

Then night came, and storm, and the path was dark, and the children shook with fear and cold, and the mother drew them close and covered them with her mantle, and the children said, "Oh, Mother, we are not afraid, for you are near, and no harm can come." And the mother observed, "This is better than the brightness of day, for I have taught my children courage."

And the morning came, and there was a hill ahead, and the children climbed and grew weary, and the mother was weary too, but she said to the children, "A little patience and we are there." So the children climbed, and when they reached the top they said, "We could not have done it without you, Mother." And the mother, when she lay down that night, looked at the stars and said, "This is a better day than the last, for my children have learned fortitude in the face of hardness. Yesterday I gave them courage, and today I have given them strength."

And the next day came strange clouds which darkened the earth—clouds of war and hate and evil, and the children groped and stumbled, and the mother said, "Look up. Lift your eyes to the Light." And the children looked and saw above the clouds an Everlasting Glory, and it guided them and brought them beyond the darkness. And that night the mother said, "This is the best day of all, for I have shown my children God."

And the days went on, and the weeks and the months and the years, and the mother grew old, and she was little and bent. But her children were tall and strong, and walked with courage. And when the way was hard, they helped their mother, and when the way was rough, they lifted her, for she was as light as a feather; and at last they came to a hill, and beyond the hill they could see a shining road and golden gates flung wide.

And the mother said: "I have reached the end of my journey. And now I know that the end is better than the beginning, for my children can walk alone, and their children after them."

And the children said, "You will always walk with us, Mother, even when you have gone through the gates."

And they stood and watched her as she went on alone, and the gates closed after her. And they said: "We cannot see her, but she is with us still. A mother like ours is more than a memory. She is a living presence."[12]

In our society today the most dangerous place for a child to be is in her mother's womb. Who would ever have thought that to be true? Too many women and parents have never known or have forgotten the promise of the Lord that children are a gift: They are the fruit of the womb.

Does this promise just happen, or are there things that we do to earn this promise? No, it doesn't just happen. For a mother to become a "living presence" she must spend time, time, and more time with her children. "Is the way long?" Yes, it is. In fact at times it seems forever.

Young mothers write letters or talk to me completely frustrated with life because the children take so much time from their day. I tell them they won't always be in that phase of their lives. Enjoy the children while they're young, because as they get older both parents and children will have new sets of difficulties.

Each phase of life has challenges that are new to us. I can vividly remember when Bob and I had five children under the age of five and I was only 21 years old. I thought I would never make it. But was it worth it? Yes, it was. I can truly say that children are a gift from God and that they are a fruit from the mother's womb.

I have found that you develop a living presence with your children if you—

- raise them at an early age to know Christ personally;
- show interest in their friends and activities;
- show them that you really love your spouse (if you are married);
- exercise fairness with them in conversation and discipline;
- let them grow up without overprotection; let them make mistakes, make decisions, and get bumps and scrapes;

- use encouraging words to lift them up;

- let them have and express different opinions from your own;

- be good role models so they will know their gender roles (boys are to become men and girls are to become women);

- be willing to clearly confess and admit your wrong doings and ask for forgiveness;

- establish firm and clear boundaries.

Proverbs 31:10-31 can help you become a capable woman. This passage is an acrostic poem exalting the honor and dignity of womanhood. In verses 30 and 31 we read, "A woman who fears the Lord . . . shall be praised. Give her the product of her hands, and let her works praise her in the gates."

Is the way long? Yes, and the way is hard. And you will be old before you reach the end of it. But the end will be better than the beginning.

Get on board, for the trip will be a blessing for you and for all those fortunate enough to be in your family!

> *Father God, thank You again for the assurance that Your plan works. As I talk to friends, see the news on the TV, and read the newspaper, I get so discouraged about having children. I truly want my children to be a gift from You and the fruit of the womb for me. In turn I also want to be a blessing in their lives. Give me the strength today to set my foot on the path of life. Amen.*

Taking Action

- Recommit your life to Christ and rededicate yourself to become a living presence to your children.

- Give each of your children a hug today and tell them how much you love them.

🌱 Tell your spouse (if you have one) of your new challenges and commitment in raising your children.

Reading On

Job 42:12,13	1 Samuel 1:8
Proverbs 22:6	Acts 2:38,39

> As a little girl was eating her dinner, the golden rays of the sun fell upon her spoon. She put the spoon to her mouth, exclaiming, "O mother! I have just swallowed a whole spoonful of sunshine!"
>
> — *B.M. Adams*

□ □ □

What Shall I Do with Jesus?

Scripture Reading: Matthew 27:11-26

Key Verse: Matthew 27:22

Pilate said to them, "Then what shall I do with Jesus who is called Christ?"

———— ❧ ————

When I was a young girl, I anxiously waited each week for one of my favorite television shows, "The $64,000 Question." A contestant would answer all kinds of questions in a multitude of categories. If he or she was successful over a period of weeks, he could arrive to the plateau of answering a series of questions which if answered correctly would award them $64,000 dollars.

I couldn't imagine that much money or that anyone could be smart enough to answer those very difficult questions. To my disappointment, a scandal broke which charged the producer of the show with leaking answers to the contestants so they could continue up the scale and build excitement for their viewers. I was really let down because I truly believed that someone was smart enough to answer all the questions of life with surety.

It wasn't until I was dating my Bob that I would be confronted by him with the most basic, fundamental, and important question in my life. After coming home one evening from a wonderful date, we were sitting on the sofa of my living room apartment when he asked me the same question that Pilate asked the crowd in today's Scripture reading: "What shall I do with Jesus who is called Christ?" I had never in my young life been asked that question. I had been raised in a Jewish family and had recently graduated from Hebrew school; Jesus wasn't a personality name to be discussed in my circle of family and friends.

I asked Bob, "What do you mean? Why do I need to answer that question? I'm a good Jewish girl, I'm not a sinner, and I have no need for Him. I believe in God."

I knew that Bob was a Christian and that he believed differently than I did, but what did Jesus have to do with it? In the quietness of that room Bob began to share with me who this Jesus was. He gave me the full gospel of the birth, the life, and the resurrection of this man named Jesus. He very lovingly shared the plan of salvation with me and told me that he would pray for me regarding the answer to the big question he had asked me. In the weeks and months that followed Bob asked my mother if he could take me to church with him. My sweet and darling mother said yes. I couldn't believe she would give me permission to go to a Christian church.

While attending the services I heard teaching from Scripture that really made me ask questions—questions I had never thought about before.

Then one night in the stillness of my bedroom I knew how to answer Bob's question, "What shall I do with Jesus who is called Christ?" At that instant I asked Jesus to come into my life, to forgive me of my sins, to become my Lord and my Messiah.

The rewards that evening were worth far more than the 64,000 dollars offered on my favorite TV show.

Over the years I have realized that this is the greatest question that any person must answer in life. However you answer that question will determine what road your life will take.

How do you answer that question?

Father God, as I look back over the years, I'm
so glad I answered that question with a big yes when

I was 16 years old. That was the foundation for all the other questions that come into my life on a daily basis. You have truly been the stability when life seems so rocky. I daily appreciate what Jesus did on the cross for me. Amen.

Taking Action

- In your journal list several of your questions. Realize that you will not always know the immediate answer to these questions.
- Turn these questions over to God in prayer and give them to Him.
- Thank God for all the questions you have answers for.
- If you do not have Jesus as your Lord, ask Him into your heart today. Pray a simple prayer asking forgiveness of sins and tell Him that you want to change direction in your life. Share this news with a friend.

Reading On

John 1:49   John 3:16
John 3:3   John 3:36

I'm going to heaven and I believe I'm going by the blood of Christ. That's not popular preaching, but I'll tell you it's all the way through the Bible and I may be the last fellow on earth who preaches it, but I'm going to preach it because it's the only way we're going to get there.

—*Billy Graham*

There Was Only One

Scripture Reading: Luke 17:11-19

Key Verse: Luke 17:15

> *One of them, when he saw that he had been healed, turned back, glorifying God with a loud voice.*

As a wife and mother who is dedicated to her family and really does things because of her love for them, there are times when I would like them to take a moment and loudly say, "Mmm, that was really a good dinner! Those peas are my favorite!" Or "Mom, thanks for washing my clothes so I always have something clean to wear to school." Have you ever longed for that token of thanks? All of us, regardless of what we do (bus driver, waitress, gardener, teacher), would like to hear "Thank you!"

I'm sure Jesus was no exception to our own human needs, since He became a man for us. He was hoping that of the ten men He had healed, more than one would come back and say, "Thank You, Jesus!" But only one came back, glorifying God with a loud voice. He was truly appreciative and knew that a miracle had been performed on him. This man also realized that an almighty God had performed this miracle, and He was going to be glorified.

I would love to have been a quiet mouse in the corner listening to the other nine men's excuses for not coming back to Jesus to say thanks. It might go like this:

- Leper number 1: Left to shop at Nordstrom's. He didn't have time.

- Leper number 2: Was late to play a round of golf. He didn't have time.

- Leper number 3: Had to rush home to mow the lawn. He didn't have time.

- Leper number 4: Had a sick grandmother and had to take her for a doctor's appointment. He didn't have time.

- Leper number 5: Had to get a haircut for church the next day. He didn't have time.

- Leper number 6: Had to take his son to a soccer game. He didn't have time.

- Leper number 7: Had to go back to the office to do some paperwork. He didn't have time.

- Leper number 8: Had to pick up a few groceries at the market. He didn't have time.

- Leper number 9: Was too embarrassed because the majority of the men weren't going back. He didn't have time.

But thank God for Leper number 10. He had time to go back and say, "Thank You, Jesus." Notice in verse 19 that Jesus said, "Rise and go your way; your faith has made you well." He was healed both physically and spiritually.

One of God's chief complaints against mankind is that they do not glorify Him as God, nor do they take the time to say "Thank You."

One of the ways we can give thanks to God for all His abundance is to have grace or a blessing at the dinner table. At an early age our children were aware that Mom and Dad took time to bless our food. As they got older they were given an opportunity to thank God in their own unique way. Our fourth grandchild, Bradley Joe, insists that we end our prayer with a catchy tone and words that say, "Amen, Amen, Amen, Amen, Amen."

A quiet time for individual or group devotions helps to instill in our family an awareness of God's blessings on our family. Somehow find your own unique way to show God that you and your family glorify Him and say thanks with a heartfelt enthusiasm.

> *Father God, I want to respond as Leper number 10 did and tell You how much I thank You for all You have done for me. I am so blessed to be one of Your children. May I never stop thanking You. You are my number one priority, and I want my life to reflect that in my daily living. Amen.*

Taking Action

 Right now take time to thank God for His forgiveness of your sins.

 Write down the names of five friends to whom you've recently said thank you for something they did for you.

 Take time to call or write three people who need to hear your thanks toward them.

Reading On

Matthew 11:25   2 Corinthians 9:15

Matthew 26:27,28   Philippians 4:6

> Let us . . . give thanks to God for His graciousness and generosity to us—pledge to Him our everlasting devotion—beseech His divine guidance and the wisdom and strength to recognize and follow that guidance.
>
> —*Lyndon B. Johnson,*
> *Thanksgiving Proclamation, 1964*

□ □ □

Be a Friend

Scripture Reading: Proverbs 18:20-24

Key Verse: Proverbs 18:24b
There is a friend who sticks closer than a brother.

A mouse one day happened to run across the paws of a sleeping lion and wakened him. The lion, angry at being disturbed, grabbed the mouse and was about to swallow him, when the mouse cried out, "Please, kind sir, I didn't mean it; if you will let me go, I shall always be grateful, and perhaps I can help you someday."

The idea that such a little thing as a mouse could help him so amused the lion that he let the mouse go. A week later the mouse heard a lion roaring loudly. He went closer to see what the trouble was and found his lion caught in a hunter's net. Remembering his promise, the mouse began to gnaw the ropes of the net and kept it up until the lion could get free. The lion then acknowledged that little friends might prove great friends.

—Aesop

Friends and friendships are unique social happenings. Often I wonder why some people are attracted to others. Is it because of common interest, past experiences, physical attraction, having children that are friends of a potential friend, or going to the same church? What is it that bonds people together? As I consider the many friends I have, I sense it's a little of all of the above. They come from various backgrounds, religions, economic levels, and educational attainment. There does, however, seem to be one common strand that runs through most of these friendships: We have a kindred spirit in the Lord.

The writer of today's Proverb gives a warning in the first part of verse 24: "A man of many friends comes to ruin." When I first read that I was confused. I thought to myself, "I thought we were to have a lot of friends, so why this warning?" But as I thought about this, a thought came to me. He was stressing that too many friends chosen indiscriminately will bring trouble, but a genuine friend sticks with you through thick and thin. When we use this criterion for a friend, we begin to thin the ranks of who are truly our friends.

I know without a doubt that several of my friends would be with me no matter what the circumstances, what day of the week, and what time of the day or night I needed help. I call these my "2 A.M. friends."

As in our Aesop story today, you never know when you will need a friend. I have found that those who have friends are themselves friendly. They go out of their way to be a friend. In order to have friends, one must be a friend.

The skill of friendship-making is a skill that we need to teach our children. We as parents have only a short window of opportunity to teach the value of positive friendships to them. Each year we have less time for our influence on them. The music, dress, dance, and jewelry selections of the world seem to pull our children from our group. While there is still time, we need to steer our youngsters to choosing the right kind of friends.

> *Father God, I thank You for the many wonder-ful friends You have given me over the years. I know how each one has been, and continues to be, a support system for me. They cry with me, laugh with me, pray with me, and hold me in all of life's*

episodes. Be with the woman reader today who lacks friends; may You reveal to her ways of developing the kind of friends that will stick closer than a brother or sister. Amen.

Taking Action

- Evaluate your friends. What does each bring to your relationship with her or him.

- Set out today to be a friend with someone.

- Plan a "tea party" and invite some friends for an afternoon gathering.

- Call or write a friend and tell her how much you enjoy her friendship.

Reading On

John 15:13	John 15:15
Proverbs 17:17	James 2:23

If a man does not make new acquaintances as he advances through life, he will soon find himself left alone. A man should keep his friendship in constant repair.

—*Samuel Johnson*

He Began a Good Work in You

Scripture Reading: Philippians 1:1-11

Key Verse: Philippians 1:6
> *I am confident of this very thing, that He who began a good work in you will perfect it until the day of Christ Jesus.*

At one point in my young married career I found my motivations to be all wrong. I really wanted to be a helpmate for Bob, but I was caught up in the pressure of trying to meet everyone's expectations, including my own. The house always had to be perfect and the children spotless. I was frustrated as a wife and mother because I was doing it all myself—100 percent from me and nothing from God. I was trying to be the perfect wife, perfect in every way. I was trying to be—

- loving
  - kind
    - a friend
      - patient
        - well-organized.

In addition to all this—

- I balanced discipline and flexibility;
  - my home was always neat and well-decorated;
    - my children were always well-behaved;

- I was serious, but I could laugh;
  - I was submissive, but not passive;
- I was full of energy and never tired;
  - my dress was proper and suitable for all occasions;
    - I could work in the garden without getting dirt under my fingernails;
  - I was always healthy;
    - and I had a close walk with God.

Needless to say, I wasn't being very effective at anything I did. I had created a superwoman image that I couldn't pull off.

During this time in my life I came across Philippians 1:6: "I am confident of this very thing, that He who began a good work in you will perfect it until the day of Christ Jesus." I realized that I was the product of God working in me and that I had three alternatives for solving my dilemma: First, I could continue trying to be superwife and supermom by doing everything myself; second, I could follow the old adage "Let go and let God," and let God do everything; or third, I could enter a balanced partnership between myself and God.

I selected the last alternative because according to Philippians 2:12,13 God was at work inside me, helping me to obey Him and to do what He wanted. God had made me a wife and a mom on purpose, and He would help me perform my role. Once I accepted this truth, a burden lifted from my life. I experienced less stress and I had a better understanding of what God wanted from me and what resources He was able to provide me. The drudgeries of homemaking became a real joy when I saw myself as a partner with God in developing godly traits in my children and creating a warm, safe nest for our family.

As I searched the Scriptures to discover my role in this partnership, I came up with three areas.

1. *Faithfulness.* According to 1 Corinthians 4:2, if I am to be a good manager of my home, I must remain faithful. Specifically, God wants me to faithfully thank Him that His plans are being fulfilled in my family. I am often impatient and want things to change right now. But God wants me to stop being concerned about His timetable and to just give thanks that He is doing His job. Over the years I have learned that if I am faithful in giving thanks, God is faithful in His part.

2. *Obedience.* It is my responsibility to act upon God's promises for my life. I can't just sit back and do nothing. Nor can I wait until all situations are perfect and safe. I must do a good job of preparation and then move ahead obediently, even if it means risking failure. Some of my best steps of growth have come after failure.

3. *Growth.* When Bob and I attended Bill Gothard's seminar several years ago he was distributing a lapel badge with the following initials: PBPGINFWMY. I was intrigued by the badge, and soon found out that the letters represented the simple message "Please be patient; God is not finished with me yet."

Yes, the Christian walk is a process of growth. I wanted to arrive instantly at the level of being a perfect wife and mother, but God showed me that my focus was to be on the lifelong process, not on arrival. If we focus on perfection we will always be disappointed because we will never achieve it. But if we focus on the process of growth we can always have hope for improvement tomorrow.

> *Father God, thank You for revealing to me that life is a process. I don't have to be superwoman or some phantom wife that society has depicted for me. You know who I am, what strengths and weaknesses I possess, and that my goal is to serve You. Please reveal to me a balance in living out life. Help those women who are in a similar state of life today. Give them the power to overcome the forces of false expectations. Amen.*

Taking Action

- List in your journal several phantoms that exist in your life.

- Beside each one, state how you are going to overcome this false expectation.

- Give your list and solutions over to the Lord in prayer.

- Be willing to believe that God has a better plan for your life.

Reading On

Philippians 2:12,13   Psalm 90:12
1 Corinthians 4:2   Matthew 6:33

When the darkness of dismay comes, endure until it is over, because out of it will come that following of Jesus which is an unspeakable joy.

— *Oswald Chambers*

Oxen and Donkeys Don't Go Together

Scripture Reading: Deuteronomy 22:1-11

Key Verse: Deuteronomy 22:10
> *You shall not plow with an ox and a donkey together.*

One evening as Bob and I came home from a date and were sitting on the sofa in my small apartment's living room, he held my face between his hands and looked me straight in the eyes. He told me that he loved me very much and that someday he would like to marry me, but he couldn't ask me to marry him. I thought that was strange, because when two people are in love why can't they be married? Then I asked "Why not?" as tears were coming down my cheeks.

Bob, in a very caring and loving way, quoted 2 Corinthians 6:14, which was deeply engraved on his heart and mind: "Do not be bound together with unbelievers; for what partnership have righteousness and lawlessness, or what fellowship has light with darkness?" (Some translations speak of not being unequally yoked together.) Then he gave me three reasons why he couldn't marry me.

First, a Christian cannot marry a non-Christian because of what unequal marriage will do to the non-Christian. There is no fellowship between light and darkness. The marriage will have a divided loyalty. Bob said, "If I promise to marry you, I am choosing to spend my life with someone who is going in a completely different direction from me. We will move farther and farther apart. I have no right to draw you into a relationship which is doomed to disharmony."

Second, a Christian can't marry an unbeliever because of what it will do to him if he disobeys God on this issue. He will compromise his standards later and disobey God again and again. Too much is at stake if he disobeys God's clear command about marriage.

I asked, "But what if I become a Christian after we're married?" Bob responded that marriage is not a mission field. God never called Christians into an unequal marriage in order to convert the unbelieving partner.

Third, an unequal marriage cannot honor God. He did not create us and redeem us so we could live for ourselves. God placed us here to glorify *Him*. And a Christian home is the only home which can truly glorify God. When a husband and wife both belong to Jesus Christ and live in obedience to Him, they provide a vital witness to the society around them.

I SAID A PRAYER FOR YOU TODAY

I said a prayer for you today,
And know God must have
heard, I felt the answer in my
heart, Although He spoke no
word. . . . I asked that He'd be
near you, At the start of each
new day, To grant you health
and blessings. And friends to
share your way. I asked for happiness for you. In all things great
and small, But it was for His loving care I prayed the most of all.

—*Margaret Gould*

In my innocence I asked, "How do I become a Christian?" And from that moment I began to ask myself if Jesus Christ was the Messiah my Jewish people were awaiting. After several months of seeking answers, I prayed one evening at bedtime, "Dear God: If You have a Son, and if Your Son is Jesus, our Messiah, please reveal Him to me!" I expected a voice to answer me immediately. But God did reveal Himself to me within a few weeks.

One Sunday morning I responded to Pastor Sailhammer's challenge to accept Jesus Christ as my personal Savior. That evening I was baptized. I was thrilled.

Because of Bob's farming background he knew experientially that you did not join two unlike animals together to plow a field. They each pull differently and plow at different paces. It creates chaos when a farmer attempts such a teaming together. The Scriptures also state clearly that believers should not be married to unbelievers, because a similar result will take place. Each party marches to a different drumbeat.

I'm so thankful that Bob had such a strong conviction as a young man. Without that I might never have been challenged to examine the claims of Jesus. I know for sure that we would not have had the same quality of marriage that we have today.

God gives certain warnings in Scripture that save His children a lot of pain down the line. If we don't heed the warnings, then we must be willing to endure the consequences of that neglect.

Scripture provides very practical teachings to those who find themselves the wives of unsaved husbands:

- Do not preach to an unsaved husband (2 Corinthians 4:4).

- Salvation is the work of the Holy Spirit (2 Peter 3:9).

- Cultivate a quiet and gentle spirit (1 Peter 3:4).

- Be submissive in your love (2 Timothy 1:7; 1 Peter 3:1).
- Pray for your husband's salvation (Acts 16:31).

Father God, to this very day I appreciate Bob's willingness to stand firm in his convictions of scriptural truths. Because of his willingness to be faithful in this area of his life, I have benefited in other decisions requiring sound biblical interpretation. Amen.

Taking Action

❦ Has this principle been a blessing in your marriage?

❦ How might you have been blessed if you had heeded this warning?

❦ If your husband is a fellow believer, thank God today for that gift.

❦ If your husband is not a fellow believer, ask God to use you in a mighty way so that your husband can see Jesus through your life.

Reading On

2 Corinthians 4:4	1 Peter 3:4
2 Peter 3:9	1 Peter 3:1

In marriage, *being* the right person is as important as *finding* the right person.

—*Wilbert Donald Gough*

Created Differently

Scripture Reading: Psalm 139:13-18

Key Verse: Psalm 139:13

> *Thou didst form my inward parts; Thou didst weave me in my mother's womb.*

A few months ago our local ABC affiliate was promoting a documentary special that reflected the latest research findings. It was going to give the viewer the latest evidence that men and women are made differently. I looked at Bob and he looked at me and we both laughed. Where had these producers been the last 2000 years?

We don't pride ourselves as intellectual geniuses, but we certainly had a grasp on this topic, even though for years the media has tried to tell us that there aren't any differences between men and women. Unfortunately, much of the Christian community has bought into this lie. A woman can't comprehend why her husband doesn't look at situations the same way she does. Why isn't he sensitive, why doesn't he like to go shopping with me, why does work seem more important to him than family?

Men and women are different in many ways: in physiology and anatomy, in thought patterns, in cultural roles and expectations. For the most part these differences are the result of God's design. Genesis 1:27 reads, "And God created man in His own image; in the image of God He created him; male and female He created them." Psalm 139:13,14 states: "Thou didst form my inward parts; Thou didst weave me in my mother's womb. I will give thanks to Thee, for I am fearfully and wonderfully made."

In these two passages we get a glimpse of God's marvelous plan in human creation. Men and women, as different as they are, are made in God's image. God called this creation good, and David said it was wonderful. A Christian husband and wife can move into their marriage relationship with the confidence that God has put each partner on the earth for a special purpose. Our differences are by God's design.

In Matthew 22:37-39 Jesus outlined simply and directly the greatest two commandments in the Scriptures: "You shall love the Lord your God with all your heart, and with all your soul, and with all your mind" and "You shall love your neighbor as yourself." These commands provide the primary guideline for responding to our differences as husband and wife.

• First, we are to love God. This implies that we accept His creation as good and agree that the male/female differences He designed are good.

• Second, when we love ourselves it means that we accept ourselves for what God has made us: a unique man or woman created for a special and different purpose than our mate.

• Third, we are to love others, particularly the mate God gave us, complete with his or her differences. Loving our mate doesn't mean changing him; that's the Holy Spirit's role. Loving our mate means understanding his differences and accepting him as he is. A loving understanding of each other as husband and wife establishes our house. Seeking to understand each other is a continuous process which leads to less anger and frustration in the relationship. We may still have difficulty with each other's actions, but at least we are growing in the understanding of why our mate does what he does.

Another scriptural guideline for dealing with differences in our marriage is Romans 12:2: "Do not be conformed to this world, but be transformed by the renewing of your mind, that you may prove what the will of God is, that which is good and acceptable and perfect." The world teaches us to stand up for our individuality and not to give in to our mate's differences. But Paul directs us not to conform to that standard, but to be transformed by the renewing of our minds. We are to let God's teaching on the blending of differences permeate our thinking and subsequently our actions.

As Christian men and women, we are (and ever will be) different. But as we take God's attitude toward our differences we will enjoy a house "filled with all precious and pleasant riches" (Proverbs 24:4). These rewards include:

- positive attitudes

- good relationships

- pleasant memories

- mutual respect

- depth of character.

We have a choice: We can live in a war zone fueled by our differences as men and women, or we can live in a house filled with the precious and pleasant riches which come from understanding and accepting our differences.

Perhaps the greatest enemy of understanding and accepting differences is pride. God hates pride, yet we seem to struggle against it in everything we do. We must break down the walls of pride which our differences erect in order to enjoy the rewards which *understanding* promises.

*Father God, thank You so much for making
man and woman so differently. Even though I think
that Bob is weird at times and I'm sure he thinks I'm*

strange, I appreciate his differences when we need to solve a problem. He doesn't get tangled up emotionally like I do and he can stand back and objectively look at what needs to be done. Thank You for creating us so differently. Amen.

Taking Action

 List three ways your husband is different from you:
- — emotionally
- — physically
- — culturally
- — spiritually

 You might ask him the same question regarding how he is different in each area from you.

 Involve your children with the same questions. Let them begin to be aware that God has created us differently—male and female.

Reading On

Genesis 1:27	Proverbs 2:1-5
Matthew 22:37-39	Romans 12:2

There is one glory of the sun,
and another glory of the moon,
and another glory of the stars;
for star differs from star in glory.

— *1 Corinthians 15:41*

Five O'Clock or
Six O'Clock

Scripture Reading: James 1:19-27

Key Verse: James 1:19,20

Let everyone be quick to hear, slow to speak, and slow to anger; for the anger of man does not achieve the righteousness of God.

———— 🐛 ————

Two of my very favorite relatives were Uncle Saul and Auntie Phyllis. For years, before Uncle Saul passed away, they would tell about a certain event and always disagree on how it happened: They didn't go by boat but flew; they didn't see the movie but the play; they served chicken, not beef; it was snowing, not sunny.

After awhile we said, "Five o'clock, six o'clock, what difference does it make?" Yet they would continue to correct each other on the details of the story. Fortunately they would smile and laugh and not take it personally, but we as outsiders knew they would never agree on anything.

Marriage experts tell us that the number one cause for divorce in America today is a lack of communication. Everyone is born with one mouth and two ears—the basic tools for communication. But possessing the physical tools for communication is not enough. Couples must learn how to use their mouths and ears properly for true communication to take place. Since God created marriage for companionship, completeness, and communication, we can be sure that He will also provide us with the resources for fulfilling His design.

There are three partners in a Christian marriage: husband, wife, and Jesus Christ. In order for healthy communication to exist between husband and wife, there must be proper communication between all three partners. If there is a breakdown in dialogue between any two members, the breakdown will automatically affect the third member of the partnership. Dwight Small says: "Lines open to God invariably open to one another, for a person cannot be genuinely open to God and closed to his mate. . . . God fulfills His design for Christian marriage when lines of communication are first opened to Him."[13] If you and your mate are having difficulty communicating, the first area to check is your individual devotional life with God.

Whenever Bob and I suffer a breakdown in relating to each other, it is usually because one of us is not talking with God on a regular basis. When both of us are communicating with God regularly through prayer and the study of His Word, we enjoy excellent communication with each other as well.

In his book *Communication: Key to Your Marriage*, Norm Wright gives an excellent definition of communication: "Communication is a process (either verbal or nonverbal) of sharing information with another person in such a way that he understands what you are saying. *Talking* and *listening* and *understanding* are all involved in the process of communication."

According to Wright, there are three elements in proper communication: talking, listening, and understanding.

Talking

Most of us have little difficulty talking. We are usually willing to give an opinion or offer advice, even when it hasn't been requested. Often our communication problems are not from talking, but from talking *too much*.

James 3:2-10 states that the human tongue can be employed for good purposes or bad. The tongue is like a rudder which can steer us into stormy or peaceful life situations.

Solomon said, "A word aptly spoken is like apples of gold in settings of silver" (Proverbs 25:11 NIV). Teaching on this passage, Florence Littauer says that our words should be like silver boxes tied with bows. I like that description because I can visualize husbands and wives giving lovely gifts like silver boxes to each other in their conversation. We are not to speak ugly words which tear down our mates, but we are to speak uplifting and encouraging words that will bring a blessing.[14]

Listening

Listening is a skill which most people haven't learned. Of Wright's three elements of communication—talking, listening, and understanding—listening is usually the trouble area. Instead of patiently hearing what our mates have to say, most of us can hardly wait until they stop talking so we can put in our two cents' worth. God gave each of us two ears, but only one mouth. Consequently we should be ready to listen at least twice as much as we speak.

Listening is the disciplined ability to savor your partner's words much like you savor and enjoy a fine meal, a thoughtful gift, lovely music, or a great book. To properly listen is to take time to digest the content of the message and to let it get under your skin and into your system. When we openly and patiently listen to our mates, we truly learn from them.

Understanding

We may speak clearly and our mates may listen intently, but if they don't understand our message, we haven't communicated very well. There are two major reasons why we fail to communicate in speaking.

- First, when we speak there is often a difference between what we mean to say and what we really say. The idea may be clear in our head, but the words we choose to express the idea may be inappropriate.

- Second, when we listen there is a difference between what we hear and what we think we hear. Perhaps the words we heard correctly conveyed the speaker's idea to everyone else, but we misunderstood them. And every time we respond to what we think we hear instead of what was actually said, the communication problem is further compounded.

One way to help clarify our communication is to repeat to our mate what we heard, and then ask, "Is that what you said?" Whenever we stop to ask that clarifying question we are helping to keep the channels of understanding open and flowing.

Many of us don't communicate because we don't believe that Jesus accepts us as we are. And since we don't feel accepted by Jesus, we do not accept ourselves and we cannot accept others and communicate with them either. We are too busy trying to shape up for God so that He will love and accept us. Communication between Christian marriage partners is a spiritual exercise. The closer we each get to God, the closer we get to each other.

Father God, You know that Bob and I have spent endless hours trying to be good communicators with each other and to others. We know how difficult, stressful, and emotional this skill is, but we also know how valuable it is to our marriage. As we look around, we see a correlation between good marriages and good communication. May we continue to have the desire to lift each other up in word and deed. Amen.

Taking Action

❧ Agree with your mate that you will say, "Five o'clock, six o'clock, what difference does it make?" when you differ on your version of the story.

❧ Another good verbiage to be used around the family is, "Is it edifying?" (a concept taken from Ephesians 4:29).

❧ Set a date night on the calendar when you and your husband can get away from the family and discuss real issues of life. Don't make it too heavy. Have fun with each other.

Reading On

James 3:2-10   Proverbs 18:13
Ephesians 4:29   Proverbs 25:11

There is a time to say nothing,
and a time to say something,
but there is not time to say
everything.

— *Hugo of Fleury*

David's Prayer of Repentance

Scripture Reading: Psalm 51:1-19

Key Verse: Psalm 51:12

> *Restore to me the joy of your salvation and grant me a willing spirit, to sustain me* (NIV).

In this psalm David pleads for forgiveness and cleansing (verses 1,2), confesses his guilt (verses 3-6), prays for pardon and restoration (verses 7-12), resolves to praise God (verses 13-17), and prays for the continued prosperity of Jerusalem (verses 18,19). This psalm elaborates David's confession of his sin with Bathsheba (2 Samuel chapters 11 and 12, with emphasis on 12:3).

This portion of Scripture highlights the highs of victory and the lows of defeat. We as sinners can appreciate how heavy David's heart was and his desire to approach his heavenly Father to ask forgiveness and to be restored in his daily walk of uprightness in the presence of God. The NIV translation of Psalm 51 reads so poetically that I thought you would like to read it with no interruptions.

> Have mercy on me, O God,
>   according to your unfailing love;
> according to your great compassion
>   blot out my transgressions.
> Wash away all my iniquity
>   and cleanse me from my sin.

David's Prayer of Repentance

For I know my transgressions,
  and my sin is always before me.
Against you, you only, have I sinned
  and done what is evil in your sight,
so that you are proved right when you speak
  and justified when you judge.
Surely I was sinful at birth,
  sinful from the time my mother conceived me.
Surely you desire truth in the inner parts;
  you teach me wisdom in the inmost place,
Cleanse me with hyssop, and I will be clean;
  wash me, and I will be whiter than snow.
Let me hear joy and gladness;
  let the bones you have crushed rejoice.
Hide your face from my sins
  and blot out all my iniquity.
Create in me a pure heart, O God,
  and renew a steadfast spirit within me.
Do not cast me from your presence
  or take your Holy Spirit from me.
Restore to me the joy of your salvation
  and grant me a willing spirit, to sustain me.
Then I will teach transgressors your ways,
  and sinners will turn back to you.
Save me from bloodguilt, O God,
  the God who saves me,
  and my tongue will sing of your righteousness.
O Lord, open my lips,
  and my mouth will declare your praise.
You do not delight in sacrifice, or I would bring it;
  you do not take pleasure in burnt offerings.
The sacrifices of God are a broken spirit;
  a broken and contrite heart,
    O God, you will not despise.

In your good pleasure make Zion prosper;
  build up the walls of Jerusalem.
Then there will be righteous sacrifices,
  whole burnt offerings to delight you;
  then bulls will be offered on your altar.

This is a confession to meditate over. Chew it up and digest it. As I go over this confession, certain words and phrases touch my inner soul. Some of them include:

- Have mercy on me
- Blot out my transgressions (sins)
- I have sinned against You
- I have a sin nature since birth
- Cleanse me and make me whiter than snow
- Let me again hear joy and gladness
- Blot out my iniquity
- Create in me a pure heart
- Renew a steadfast spirit within me
- Don't cast me away
- Restore my joy of Your salvation
- Give me a willing spirit
- I will teach others of Your ways
- Save me from bloodguilt
- My tongue will sing of Your righteousness
- Open my lips and mouth for praise
- Give me a broken and contrite heart.

As you examine this confession you see a man who has been broken and begs for restoration. I have never been to the depths of David's despair, but my sins have brought me to the place where I cry out to God, "Please forgive me, a helpless sinner."

First John 1:9 has been a great restoration promise for me. It reads, "If we confess our sins, He is faithful and righteous to forgive us our sins and to cleanse us from all unrighteousness."

Don't let the sun set on any unconfessed sin. Don't delay to confess because it will build up a callus around your heart and make repentance harder to deal with.

As I see and hear news stories that deal with crime, I see few people who confess and ask for forgiveness. They are always looking to find excuses:

- My father died when I was young
- My home was very dysfunctional
- My mother took drugs
- My father drank a lot
- I had a bad neighborhood
- My schools were underfunded.

Excuse after excuse, but few people want to say as David did, "Against you, you only, have I sinned; please forgive me of my transgressions."

David realized that after confession there would be joy again. If you are burdened down today with a heavy heart because of unconfessed sin in your life, claim 1 John 1:9 and be restored to the joy of your salvation. God will create a pure heart within you.

Father God, I want to give You all of my known and unknown sins today. I don't want to leave Your presence with any unconfessed sin in my life. I want to go away with a clean heart and have Your joy of forgiveness in me. Only by Your grace have You protected me from the ugliness of sin. Please be with the ladies who read today's psalm, so that they too will know of Your grace, love, and forgiveness. Amen.

Taking Action

- ❧ Meditate on Psalm 51.
- ❧ Study this passage and jot down in your journal the observations you make.
- ❧ Say a prayer to God confessing all of your sins.
- ❧ Go away with a song in your heart.

Reading On

Luke 18:13   Ephesians 2:8,9
John 3:16   Romans 3:23

It is the duty of nations as well
as of men to confess their sins
and transgressions in humble
sorrow, yet with assured hope
that genuine repentance will
lead to mercy and pardon.

—Abraham Lincoln

Keep Your Nest Warm

Scripture Reading: Genesis 2:18-25

Key Verse: Genesis 2:21

The Lord God caused a deep sleep to fall upon the man, and he slept; then He took one of his ribs and closed up the flesh at that place.

———— ❦ ————

When God created Eve out of Adam's rib, He equipped her with unique characteristics which complemented her husband. Apparently one of the characteristics God invested in Eve and her female descendants was the nesting instinct. Bob and I have noticed that most of the women we meet in seminars have a desire to create and maintain a warm, attractive home for themselves, their husbands, and their children. Though we express it in many different ways, we women seem to be more home-oriented than our husbands.

The changing role of women in our society has tended to submerge the nesting instinct, and today's female doesn't operate much like Grandma did. Women today don't cook, clean, iron, or mother like previous generations. *Careers* are more popular with women, and many are forced to work to support an affluent lifestyle. In many cases a couple cannot even buy a home unless both partners are working full-time.

Children are often the neglected victims of the woman's misplaced nesting instinct. Childcare centers and extended day schools are almost a necessity in our society. One preschool teacher I met said the children she cares for are with her an average of 11 hours a day!

Today's mothers are trusting other people to raise their children. Mom picks up her kids after a hard day's work, races through the fast-food restaurant on the way home, and then kicks off her shoes and passes out. There is no time for nesting and mothering. Older latchkey kids come home to an empty house where potato chips and television are their best friends. Whatever happened to homemade cookies and milk and warm comments like "Tell me about your day" and "May I help you with your homework?"

Today a homemaker committed to nesting and mothering is often seen as inferior to a career-oriented woman. If she teaches someone else's children she is given the title of teacher; if she teaches her own children she is just a mother. If she chooses paint, wallpaper, and fabric for others she is an interior decorator; if she decorates her own home she's just a homemaker. If she professionally cares for the bumps and bruises of other people she's a nurse; if she cares for her own children's physical needs she is only a mom doing her job. Mothers employ the skills of many professions but usually receive much less recognition than professional women.

I loved my role as a wife and mother and grandmother, and I continually endeavored to keep our nest warm. I worked at organizing my time to care for the children so I had time for other activities. It was important to me to exchange recipes, be involved in church, and be available for Bob's needs. Caring for my family was exciting to me, but I didn't depend on them for all my strokes. Reaching out to other activities brought a balance to my life. As the children got older I taught a Bible study and built a thriving business in my home. But my activities were always subject to my priorities of seeking the Lord first, being a helpmate to Bob, guiding our children, and keeping our nest clean.

My friend Barbara is a master at making her family's nest a joyful and comfortable place. When her family goes on vacation, Barbara takes her nest with her. Upon arrival at the hotel or motel she pulls out a checkered tablecloth, candles, crackers, and cheese. She brings flowers to place by the bed and a perfumed candle or spray to enhance the bathroom. When her children were small Barbara brought games, popcorn, crayons, and each child's favorite pillow, toy, or "blankie" on each trip. Barbara keeps building her nest wherever the family goes. The effort required isn't great—throwing a few extra things in a suitcase or backpack—but the effort expended is sure worth the positive results.

The apostle Paul wrote: "Older women likewise are to be reverent in their behavior, not malicious gossips, nor enslaved to much wine, teaching what is good, that they may encourage the young women to love their husbands, to love their children" (Titus 2:3,4). As a young wife and mother my heart's desire was to be the kind of younger woman that Paul described in these verses. I was a new Christian and I knew I needed the positive influence and teaching of older, more mature women. I began to search out this type of older woman who could teach me all about being a maker of a home. Over the years I have had many mentors help me grow into where I am today. And God has now given me that role to encourage women all over this country to be a role model in keeping their nest warm.

Father God, thank You for all the women You have given me to help light my path. Without them I know I would not be the woman I am today. As You give me the opportunity to be a Titus woman, may the women who come to my seminars see Your Son, Jesus, in a real, true-to-life experience. I'm so appreciative for all You do for me and my family. I really do love my nest and all those who are part of it. Amen.

Taking Action

 List in your journal three to five women who have been Titus women for you. After each name write what they have contributed to your life.

 If they are still alive, take a moment to call them on the phone or to write a note and say, "Thank you for what you have done for me." This will do wonders for you and they will be greatly encouraged as well.

 Buy some fresh flowers and have them in the nest when your family arrives home this evening.

Reading On

Proverbs 31:27,28	Titus 2:3-5
Psalm 139:23	Psalm 73:26

The Christian home is the Master's workshop, where the processes of character-molding are silently, lovingly, faithfully, and successfully carried on.

— *Richard Monckton Milnes*

Living by God's Surprises

Scripture Reading: James 1:2-12

Key Verse: James 1:2

Consider it all joy, my brethren, when you encounter various trials.

Throughout Scripture we read of victory through troubles and suffering. Helmut Thielicke, the great German pastor and theologian, testified to this kind of victory during the horrors of World War II.

When Thielicke said, "We live by God's surprises," he had personally suffered under the Nazis. As a pastor he wrote to young soldiers about to die; he comforted mothers and fathers and children after the bombs killed their loved ones. He preached magnificent sermons week after week as bombs blew apart his church and the lives and dreams of his parishioners. He spoke of God not only looking in love at His suffering people, weeping with them as they were surrounded by flames, but of God's hand reaching into the flames to help them, His own hand scorched by the fires.

From the depths of suffering and the wanton destruction during the Nazi regime, Thielicke held out a powerful Christian hope. To Germans disillusioned by the easily manipulated faith of their fathers, he quoted

Peter Wust: "The great things happen to those who pray. But we learn to pray best in suffering."

Prayer, suffering, joy, and the surprises of God...they are all tightly enmeshed. But most shrink from the above statement, seeing suffering as the surest killer of both joy and "great things."

When we are rightly related to God, life is full of joy-ful uncertainty and expectancy...we do not know what God is going to do next; He packs our lives with surprises all the time.

What a strange idea: "joyful uncertainty." Most of us view uncertainty as cause for anxiety, not joy. Yet this call to expectancy rings true. The idea of standing on tiptoe to see what God is going to do next can trans-form our way of seeing. Prayers go maddeningly unan-swered as well as marvelously fulfilled. Prayer becomes the lens through which we begin to see from God's perspective.[15]

When I read of men or women with such courage, I feel so insignificant when I approach God each day in prayer. It's hard for me to grasp the height of joy that these personalities of God must have experienced during this time in history. When James writes, "Consider it all joy, my brethren, when you en-counter various trials, knowing that the testing of your faith produces endurance; and let endurance have its perfect result, that you may be perfect and complete, lacking in nothing" (James 1:2-4), I realize that life will be a challenge.

Who said that the Christian walk will be easy? These pas-sages and events make me realize that there will be surprises when we live for God. We in America have it pretty easy com-pared to the rest of the world. Throughout Jesus' ministry He shared with His followers that there would be a cost if they fol-lowed Him.

Thielicke, along with the other historical pillars of the church, give testimony that prayer becomes the lens through which we begin to see life from God's perspective.

I hear many people ask in a harsh tone, "Well, I'm going to ask God when I get to heaven why He did. . . . !" But I think we will stand in such awe in His presence that such questions will be meaningless, because then we will see history from God's point of view.

Wouldn't it be wonderful if when we got out of bed each morning we stood on our tiptoes to see what God is going to do today? We would joyfully look forward to see what God is going to do next. When we see life like that, our cup will surely "run over" and life will be joyful. Our cup will always be full, and as we pour out its contents God will give us new refreshment to fill it full again. Lord, I want to experience that joy!

> *Father God, I want to live life so that I truly live expectantly for Your surprises. I want to tiptoe to see Your mysteries unveiled for me. May I learn to see life from Your end, and forget about all of man's wonderful knowledge, even though it is magnificent. Give me depth in my prayer life to match that of Helmut Thielicke. Here is a man who undoubtedly saw Jesus face-to-face with a true joy of assurance. Amen.*

Taking Action

- ❧ Evaluate the quality and quantity of your prayer life. How can it be strengthened?

- ❧ Be willing to stand on your tiptoes to see what God is going to do next in your life. What do you think you might see?

- ❧ How will you react to it? What will you do for support?

Reading On

Romans 8:28   James 1:2-12
Matthew 6:33   1 Corinthians 10:13

There are three ways that prepare us for life's trials. One is the Spartan way that says, "I have strength within me to do it, I am the captain of my soul. With the courage and will that is mine, I will be master when the struggle comes." Another way is the spirit of Socrates, who affirmed that we have minds, reason, and judgment to evaluate and help us cope with the enigmas and struggles of life. The Christian way is the third approach. It doesn't exclude the other two, but adds, "You don't begin with yourself, your will, or your reason. You begin with God, who is the beginning and the end."

— *Lowell R. Ditzen*

I'm Too Sick

Scripture Reading: Romans 8:18-30

Key Verse: Romans 8:28

We know that God causes all things to work together for good to those who love God, to those who are called according to His purpose.

———— ❦ ————

It was a women's retreat I was looking forward to in February, to be held at a retreat center in Fall City, Washington. We arrived safely and on time; it was a drizzly day but it felt good to be away from dry Southern California.

As usual, the women were excited and arrived anxious for a fun-filled spiritual weekend. After two sessions on Friday evening, by 10:30 P.M. I was tired. I was in our cabin, which also housed the summer camp nurses (and looked like they needed a little nursing themselves), I anxiously fell into bed for a much-needed rest.

Two hours later I was sick with what I think was a good dose of food poisoning, although no one got sick but me. All night I spent time in the small, musty bathroom. By morning my Bob was very concerned about my strength to speak at three more sessions on Saturday. "I'll be fine," I kept reassuring him. But by 9:30 A.M. I knew there was no way I could pull myself up to speak.

"Maybe I could do it for you," my Bob suggested. "Of course you can, what a great idea!" I responded. Bob met with the retreat leaders and they were thrilled that he could fill in for me. During that morning session Bob spoke on his book

Your Husband, Your Friend. The session lasted almost two hours, and the women were hanging on his every word. What a treat to get a man's perspective on women, marriage, and relationships!

But the best was yet to come. By noon I was able to clean up pretty well and down a bit of soup and crackers. The afternoon sessions went well as I sat on a stool and finished the retreat with the Lord's strength.

Many of the women came up to me and shared how Bob's message touched them and answered questions they had always had about marriage and men.

As Janet approached me she said, "Emilie, I'm so sorry you were sick today, but if that's what it took for your Bob to speak, I'm so thankful because his message just saved my marriage. I came this weekend to get away and had decided I was leaving my husband as soon as I got back home. But today gave me understanding and hope. I'm going home to try harder and put my heart into a commitment we made years ago." Was it worth getting sick? You bet! Did God work all things together as our Scripture for today states? You bet!

In over 20 years of speaking that was the only time I ever missed a speaking engagement. God knew what Janet needed to hear and He brought it about to save a marriage.

> *Father God, how we thank You that when situations seem so difficult You are able to give us strength in our weakness, to change the impossible to the possible. Help us to keep on keeping on when our marriage relationship seems to be off the track; help us to get back on track and do our part to love our mate through You. Amen.*

Taking Action

❧ List two things you can do to help build your relationship with the one you love.

❦ Say a prayer today for your husband's needs in his awesome responsibility as the head of the family.

❦ Praise the one you love for one of his good qualities.

Reading On

Genesis 50:20   Proverbs 15:11
Romans 8:31-39   Matthew 10:29-31

He who does not believe that
God is above all is either a fool
or has no experience of life.

— *Statius Caecilius*

☐ ☐ ☐

I Will Be with Your Mouth

Scripture Reading: Exodus 4:10-12

Key Verse: Exodus 4:12

> *Now then go, and I, even I, will be with your mouth, and teach you what you are to say.*

Because of the turmoil in my home as a child, I decided I would not speak, in fear that I would say the wrong thing. I became quiet and would grasp my mother's leg in order to hide from people. I didn't want to be around people; I was afraid of my own family members and certainly strangers.

My father had a major drinking problem that put everyone on pins and needles. Everyone watched what he or she would say, because Daddy would get mad very easily and make life miserable to the messenger who said the wrong thing or in the wrong way.

I was this way until I got into high school and found myself being liked by my fellow students. As a junior I had the female lead in our senior play, "Best Foot Forward." My success in this performance began to instill in me some self-confidence.

It was also at this time that I met my Bob, who made me feel safe to be around him and his loving family. But I was very quiet and reserved, for fear that I might say the wrong thing. Bob would always say, "Emilie, speak up—you've got to tell me your thoughts on this," but I was very hesitant to express myself, fearing that I would say the wrong thing.

I Will Be with Your Mouth

It wasn't until I was in my late twenties, when I signed up for a Christian women's retreat in Palm Springs, that I realized God had a speaking program for my life. Since the women of my church knew that I came from a Jewish faith, they asked me if I would give a three-minute testimony at the retreat. I felt like Moses in Exodus 4:10: "Please, Lord, I have never been eloquent, neither recently nor in time past, nor since Thou has spoken to thy servant; for I am slow of speech and slow of tongue." Then the Lord said to me as to Moses: "Who do you think made your mouth? Is it not I the Lord?"

So I reluctantly said, "Yes, I'll do it." I wasn't sure what I would say or how I would say it, but I had confidence that my Lord and God would be by my side.

Our key verse for today gave me great strength. God said to Moses: "Now then go, and I, even I, will be with your mouth, and teach you what you are to say." That was over 35 years ago, and He still goes before me, giving me the words to say and teaching me from His Word.

I can honestly say that God will be with your mouth. I travel all over this continent sharing with women of all denominations the words He has given me to say. Along with the spoken word, He has also entrusted me with writing over 22 books, with well over a million books in print.

As a little girl who was afraid to speak I didn't have the faintest idea that God would use me to touch the lives of thousands through the spoken and written word. It only happened when God saw a willingness in my spirit to be used by Him.

My testimony was so well-received by those in the audience that I received many invitations to go to their local clubs to share my story. Of course, I had to expand it beyond the original three minutes to at least a 30-minute presentation, but God richly provided the words to say.

Am I still nervous when I get up to speak? Yes—every time. I still have to rely upon Him each time I speak to give me a peace and calm before I begin. I often wonder as I look out on the faces of my audience, "Why me, Lord? There are many better speakers and writers than I am." But He always answers back, "Now then go, and I will be with your mouth and teach you what to say."

> *Father God, I am amazed that You have been able to use me—an ordinary wife, mother, and grandmother. You continue to amaze me in how You take the ordinary and make it extraordinary. May I always be willing to share my story as long as there are people who want to hear it. The "bouquet of flowers" is laid at Your feet each night. You are to receive all the glory. Amen.*

Taking Action

- Are you holding back saying yes to God because of fear?
- In what ways?
- How can you turn your "no" answers into "yes" answers?
- Start with one "yes" answer, then watch how God will use your willingness to be used.

Reading On

Psalm 8:2   Matthew 15:11
Proverbs 26:28   Romans 10:10

He who indulges in liberty of speech will hear things in return which he will not like.

—Terrence

Tea at Nordstrom's

Scripture Reading: Colossians 4:1-6

Key Verse: Colossians 4:2
Devote yourselves to prayer, keeping alert in it with an attitude of thanksgiving.

I met some of my dearest friends while we lived in Newport Beach, California. Although we were there for only four years, it was a time of major spiritual growth in my life. The Tuesday morning prayer group taught me to pray without thee's and thou's and to communicate with my Lord as though He were sitting in the room having tea with us. I loved my Newport Beach years and the closeness I had with those Titus women.

Leaving to move to Riverside was a difficult change for me. Two weeks in our new town brought a phone call from a young mom who said she heard I was lonely and said she wanted to meet me. That meeting became a friendship that has lasted over 25 years. Her name is Vonis Waugh, and although she moved to Oregon we still maintain a very special friendship.

Recently, upon hearing that Vonis was coming to town to visit family, four of us friends decided to meet Vonis for a quick teatime at the courtyard of our local Nordstrom's department store. Two people brought candles and we ordered latte, tea, or coffee. Since it was just before Christmas none of us had much time, but it was a reconnecting of friendships, if only for 90 minutes.

Vonis complained of a pain in her stomach that had been a source of irritation for several weeks. We all gave her our own diagnoses, which ranged from ulcers to a parasite. Two weeks later Vonis called to tell us she had cancer in the form of a tumor the size of a football on her aorta artery.

Now we had to deal with this devastating news. No one knew what the next several months held in store for Vonis: tests, chemotherapy, hair loss, weight loss, depression, fear, and much more. But the treatment was working and Vonis was responding as she was surrounded with love, prayers, hope, and positive input.

Then came her next visit to Riverside, and six of us joined together at Julie's home for afternoon tea with the one we loved so dearly. The time was fun as we laughed over her bald head, long surgery scar, and cute wig. We all tried it on and laughed some more. Stories were told of old times, family, and even household pets.

But my spirit was heavy as I thought why we were here. Was it just to have meaningful conversation? I don't think so. Laughing and loving, yes, but what about our friend, who inside was worried about her life, her children, and her grandchildren that she may never see grow up? We needed to pray for a miracle for Vonis, her doctors, her health, her family, her future, and her difficult decisions.

Gathering all together, we had a circle of prayer—not too long, just enough to cover and surround her with our loving prayers. Tears flowed, hugs followed, and peace came to all of us. At this writing Vonis is doing well. The tumor has shrunk to the size of a golf ball, but still the unknown lies ahead.

Women, today we must be in touch with the needs of our friends and those we hold close to our hearts. We need to listen as they talk and to pray as we listen.

I have Vonis and her family's photo on the door of our refrigerator. Each time I open that door I pray for her. It could be 20 times a day. Our verse today says to devote ourselves to prayer. Although we are all busy women, we can devote our hearts to prayer with an attitude of thanksgiving as we come and go in our daily business. How faithful God is!

> *Father God, help me to be reminded daily to bring before You those who hurt, are ill, and are spiritually weak. Bring to my mind today that friend who needs a special touch from You, our Heavenly Father. Thank You. Amen.*

Taking Action

- 🍂 Place a photo, handprint, or note on your refrigerator as a reminder to pray for a friend.
- 🍂 Take time to drop a note to someone who needs a special encouragement.
- 🍂 Remember to thank God for His goodness.
- 🍂 Have a cup of tea with a friend.

Reading On

Luke 6:12   Romans 12:12
Acts 6:4   Philippians 4:6

🍂

Prayer is for the religious life what original research is for science—by it we get direct contact with reality. . . . We pray because we were made for prayer, and God draws us out by breathing Himself in.

— *P.T. Forsyth*

🍂

Seek His Thoughts

Scripture Reading: Isaiah 55:6-13

Key Verse: Isaiah 55:8

"My thoughts are not your thoughts, neither are your ways My ways," declares the Lord.

Suppose a man should find a great basket by the wayside, carefully packed, and upon opening it he should find it filled with human thoughts—all the thoughts which had passed through one single brain in one year or five years. What a medley they would make! How many thoughts would be wild and foolish, how many weak and contemptible, how many mean and vile, how many so contradictory and crooked that they could hardly lie still in the basket. And suppose he should be told that these were all his *own* thoughts, children of his own brain; how amazed he would be, and how little prepared to see himself as revealed in those thoughts! How he would want to run away and hide, if all the world were to see the basket opened and see his thoughts![16]

Compared to the thoughts of God, we humans seem so frail. I can't imagine being exposed for the lowliness of my thoughts. I'm sometimes amazed that I could even think of such things. At times I think, "God, why did You permit that plane to crash, or why was it necessary for that murder to take place?" At times I want to crawl inside God's mind and see how it functions and how He thinks. Then I realize that He is the potter and I am the clay. His thoughts are so much higher than mine.

It must really be frustrating for a genius with a 200-plus IQ not to be able to outthink God. (I don't have that problem, since I'm nowhere near that level of thought!) But still I wonder about God's thought power.

In Philippians 4:8 Paul gives us some idea of God's level of thought process. He tells us to think on these things:

- Whatever is true
- Whatever is honorable
- Whatever is right
- Whatever is pure
- Whatever is lovely
- Whatever is of good report.

If there is any excellence and if anything worthy of praise, let your mind dwell on these things. Then in verse 9 he gives us some action:

- What you have learned, received, heard, and seen in me—
- Practice these things.
- Then the God of peace will be with you.

As Christians we are all models that people watch to see what God is like. They are watching and hearing what we have to say about life. Either they accept our level of thought or they reject it by what they have learned, received, heard, and seen in us.

We want to be a reflection of God: As people see us in action, do they see what this Christian walk is all about? Do our children and those around us ask, "Have I ever seen a Christian?" Or do they know absolutely that they have seen a Christian when they look at us?

If people were to find our "thought basket" on the wayside, what kind of flowers would they pull out?

> *Father God, thank You for challenging me in this area of thoughts. Let me focus on pure thoughts that will stimulate me to be more Christlike. When I have a choice between two levels of thought, give me the strength and courage to take the higher road. Help women who read today's thoughts to be challenged to think upon the good things of life. May we all raise our level of thought. Amen.*

Taking Action

❧ Evaluate your thought life. What do you see?

❧ What do others see?

❧ What do you like?

❧ What do you want to change?

❧ How will you change?

Reading On

Galatians 5:19-21	Psalm 94:11
Galatians 5:22,23	Matthew 15:16-20

If you would voyage Godward, you must see to it that the rudder of thought is right.

—W.J. Dawson

Blessed Assurance

Scripture Reading: Psalm 37:1-40

Key Verse: Psalm 37:1-40

Read and meditate on each verse today.

I don't know if you're anything like I am, but when I look at the local news events on television and in the newspaper, I see very little hope for the future. I get concerned for my children and grandchildren, and even for my great-grandchildren. I see a moral decay from what I cherished by being raised in the fifties. When I go by a high school, visit a mall, listen to the music of the youth, see the art of the masses, or witness the violence of the movies, I scream in my soul, STOP!

Then the Lord brings before me Psalm 37. In this passage David exhorts the righteous to trust in the Lord. Even when it looks like evil will overpower righteousness, God never abandons His children (verse 25). Though they may experience the heartaches of a sinful, fallen world, God's children are never forsaken. In fact, His blessings will extend to the next generation (verse 26).

During my quiet time with the Lord in this particular psalm, certain key phrases comfort my soul:

- *Do not fret*, be not envious (verse 1).

- *Trust* in the Lord, cultivate faithfulness (verse 3).

- *Delight* yourself in the Lord, He will give you abundantly (verse 4).

- *Commit* your way to Him, trust also in Him (verse 5).
- *Rest* in the Lord, wait patiently (verse 7).
- *Cease* from anger, do not fret (verse 8).
- The *humble* will inherit the land (verse 11).
- *Depart* from evil (verse 27).
- *Wait* for the Lord (verse 34).

Then in verses 39 and 40 we read of the great blessings we receive as children of God: "The salvation of the righteous is from the Lord; He is our strength in time of trouble. And the Lord helps them and delivers them; He delivers them from the wicked and saves them, because they take refuge in Him."

I'M DRINKING FROM THE SAUCER

. . . If God gives me strength and courage, When the way grows steep and rough, I'll not ask for other blessings—I'm already blessed enough. May I never be too busy, To help bear another's load. I'm drinking from the saucer, 'Cause my cup has overflowed!

—*Author Unknown*

As I leave my prayer closet I am again able to face the negative issues of the day because David took time centuries ago to write this poetic psalm of comfort.

Father God, again You come to comfort me in today's psalm. You give me assurance that righteousness does deflect evil, and that Your promises are as true today as they were centuries ago. Let me dwell on these significant words from this passage: TRUST, DELIGHT, COMMIT, REST, BE HUMBLE, WAIT. I ask that You give comfort to the ladies today as they bring their cares to You. Amen.

Taking Action

- Underline in your Bible those action words that give you direction. For example: TRUST, DELIGHT, COMMIT, etc.

- Write one of these key verses on a three-by-five card. Put it in a special place where you will see it several times a day.

- Memorize this verse.

Reading On

Proverbs 3:31	Proverbs 24:19,20
Proverbs 23:17	Psalm 62:8

For God to explain a trial would be to destroy its object, which is that of calling forth simple faith and implicit obedience.

— *Alfred Edersheim*

The Work of Our Hands

Scripture Reading: Psalm 90:12-17

Key Verse: Psalm 90:17b
Confirm for us the work of our hands; yes, confirm the work of our hands.

For many years I struggled with the idea of worth in my work. I didn't have an advanced college degree and I was a homemaker with five children. I was always tired, with little energy for anything else—including romancing my husband. I didn't have a good handle on who I was as a person. I found myself saying to myself:

- You aren't worth much.

- You didn't have a career.

- Your job is so mundane.

- Anyone can do what you do.

- I don't have enough energy to do anything else.

- I'm stuck in a rat race with no place to go.

Over and over these thoughts went through my head. As you can suspect, I wasn't too exciting to be around!

I'm sure many readers of today's passage feel they have little worth in their hands. They have been browbeaten into thinking that life is fleeting by and they are being left behind. During this period in my life I was involved in a small Bible study with a few godly women who shared with us young ladies two passages of Scripture that changed my life.

One was Proverbs 31, which talked about the virtuous woman, and the other was Titus 2:4,5, which describes a wife's core role as "husband lover" and "child lover." These two sections of Scripture gave me the tools I needed to establish priorities and roles in making lifestyle decisions. I soon realized that this whole concept of work and worth was very complex and that there was no right answer to fit all situations. I realized that each woman and each family has to determine what is best for them, using biblical guidelines.

As I looked at Titus 2:4,5 I realized that God wanted me to be a lover of my husband and children. This was refreshing to me because I had looked at all these drudgeries as an end unto themselves, not as a means to fulfilling one of my primary roles as a woman. But now I found my attitude toward this work changing. I was beginning to do it out of love rather than obligation.

Once you see, you appreciate
and then you become inspired.
—*Alexandria Stoddard*

I also realized that I did more than fulfill this role, but the role gave me some structure and direction. Up to this point in our marriage I had been experiencing frustration and disappointment because I had no direction in marriage.

The Proverbs 31 passage also made me realize that the ideal Hebrew woman handled many activities outside the home. But even while these extra activities were going on she remained focused on her husband, children, and home. Her husband can trust her, the passage says, because "she does him good and not evil all the days of her life" (verse 12).

With this new information I began to shift my focus from simply doing tasks to becoming a lover of my husband and children. To this day my core focus remains in this area of my life. Even though I have gone way beyond those early beginnings, I come across countless women who don't know about or aren't willing to perform the basic focus for a married woman: being a lover of their husband and children.

When I began to change my focus, I began to realize what today's key verse, Psalm 90:17b, was addressing: "Confirm for us the work of our hands; yes, confirm the work of our hands."

What's in it for me as a woman? Proverbs 31:28,29 gives me my blessing: "Her children rise up and bless her; her husband also, and he praises her, saying, 'Many daughters have done nobly, but you excel them all.'"

When my children and husband rise up and call me blessed, then I truly know that many years ago I made the right choice when I decided to be a lover of my husband and children. Without a doubt I know that God has confirmed the work of my hands.

> *Father God, thank You again for sending me Titus women at a young age to help me focus my role as a wife and mother. As I stand before You today I'm assured that I made the right decision. I know that many women are confused about their role as a woman. May they somehow grasp this lifesaving concept of being a lover of their husband and children first, and then other opportunities will be opened to them. Amen.*

Taking Action

❦ How has God confirmed the worth of your works? Write in your journal.

❦ If you're not sure, think about this thought: "Are you a lover of your husband and children?" Yes or no?

🍏 If yes, how do you manifest this love in your home? If no, how can you manifest it in your home? What changes will be necessary?

Reading On

Proverbs 31:28,29   Psalm 8:3
Titus 2:4,5   Psalm 111:3

I am beginning to see that the things that really matter take place not in the boardrooms but in the kitchens of the world.

—*Gary Sledge*

The Heart of the Home

Scripture Reading: Proverbs 19:1-8

Key Verse: Proverbs 19:8

He who gets wisdom loves his own soul; he who keeps understanding will find good.

———— ❦ ————

In another translation we read, "Do yourself a favor and learn all you can; then remember what you've learned and you will prosper" (TEV).

Today we are returning to a new traditionalism. We are looking at our past mistakes and beginning to see what we can do to correct them in order to become the women that God uniquely created us to be. Yes, we're going back to tradition, but we will do it in a new way. We'll take on the mystique of the feminine woman, being a lady for whom men will open doors—not the "too-tired-for-sex" woman, but the woman who is beautiful inside and has charm that a man desires.

How are we going to do this? By changing our values from straw and sticks to gold and silver and by building a strong foundation of faith in God's Word (1 Corinthians 3:12).

Women, we are the mortar that holds together our homes and families. We set the thermostat in our homes. Proverbs 14:1 says that homes are made by the wisdom of women but are destroyed by foolishness. Yes, we've been foolish in some areas; we've grown and learned from that, and now we're ready to commit ourselves to making positive changes.

The Heart of the Home

My mother was a beautiful example of how the woman is the heartbeat of her home. When I was six years old my mother made me a green-and-white gingham dress with puffy sleeves, a full gathered skirt with pockets, and white heart buttons. She had a treadle Singer sewing machine. I loved to watch the rhythm of Mama's touch with her feet to make it sew. I also loved that dress. It fit so perfectly, the skirt twirled just right, and it had a nice big hem in it so I could wear it for a long time.

My mother was quite a seamstress; her father had been a tailor in Brooklyn, New York, and he had to have perfection in his garments. So my dress was well-made. At first I could only wear it on special occasions, and absolutely could not play in it.

One of my favorite times as a little girl was when my aunt and uncle came to visit us, and I got to wear my green gingham dress. One Sunday they were late in arriving and I got tired of waiting, so I went out to play—only to slip and fall into a pile of dog toot.

My dress was all I could think of as I ran home smelling very bad. But Mama was great. She pulled off my dress, washed me and the dress, and assured me the dress would be fine. But the episode took the newness out of that dress, and soon the green gingham dress became a school dress.

I grew and the hem had to be let down. Mama sewed a band of rickrack over the hemline so it wouldn't look as if it had been altered. And I was to change my dress after school. I always wanted to wear that dress, so Mama made me a new one for a best dress in the same style as my green gingham dress, but with a different fabric. Yet it just wasn't the same as my original green gingham dress.

I was growing, and my favorite dress, now with three rows of rickrack, became too short to wear. Mama said it would make a fine play dress with slacks underneath. So I wore it on Saturdays to ride my bike down to the beach. When I was eight years old I finally had to give up my green gingham dress to the rag box.

But my mother taught me how to sew, and one of my first projects was to make an apron. Out came the green gingham dress from the rag box. We cut off the gathered skirt, added a waistband and ties (pockets were already there), and presto! The dress became an apron. There was still some fabric left over, and with this Mama and I made pot holders.

I loved that apron, and Mama and I both wore it proudly as she taught me how to cook and clean. The pockets were big and handy to hold tidbits of trash as I cleaned each little room. What with cooking and cleaning, however, the apron began to get stained and a bit tattered. Unfortunately, even aprons are outgrown after a time, so back into the rag box it went.

It reappeared later, however, torn into pieces. The soft fabric made fine cloths for dusting and wiping up. One day I saw my gingham dress swishing across the floor in a rag mop. Mama made our mops out of old rags, and they worked very well. The white heart buttons popped up on several dresses after that, and also on flannel nighties. After years of continued use, I still have two of those heart buttons, 46 years later!

Heart in the home is created by teaching, delegating, and being there. We need to be there for our families. When Jenny got a splinter, had a fever, tried out for the swim team, was rejected by friends, had hair that didn't fall right, broke up with a boyfriend, and planned her wedding—I was there.

My mother became a single parent after my father died. She worked far into the night, and during all her years until she died at age 78, she remained the heart of our home. Through all the abuse, alcohol-related problems, low finances, and anger in our home, Mama remained the soft, gentle-spirited woman. During her later years she lived in a senior-citizen building in a tiny efficiency apartment. Yet she had a wreath of flowers on her front door and a few fresh daisies or pansies on the table, and she always had a cup of tea ready for anyone who knocked.

What can we do to repair the brokenness of our homes, hearts, health, marriage, relationships, and children? We can begin by looking at the 8760 hours we have each year and reducing the 70 percent of stress in our lives that is caused by disorganization. If we sleep an average of eight hours per day, that equals 2920 hours a year. We then work about 2000 hours, which gives us 3840 hours to wash, iron, plan and prepare food, clean, attend Little League or soccer games or music recitals, keep doctor appointments, help with homework, and watch television. About 37 hours a week is what it takes to accomplish our domestic chores. If we work outside our homes, how can we be there to do all that? There is no time left for us or for any interaction with our family.

Our survival lies in three areas.

- *Delegation.* Women, we can't do it alone. Super Mom must go out the window. Call a family meeting and share with them your need for help and how they can help you. I know your family will come through. Prepare ahead of time a list of areas in which they can help to relieve the stress from your life.

- *Dialogue.* Continue to share your stress feelings and allow your family to share with you. As busy as we all are, it is important to communicate back and forth about our feelings concerning teachers, schoolwork, friends, and (especially) God.

- *Interaction.* There is much we can teach our children as we work side by side with them. When the children bake cookies with me, or as we make a salad, mow the lawn, wash a car, clean the bathroom, change the linens, rake leaves, and shovel snow together, we are a team. It is amazing what I found out about my children and their feelings as we worked together. I was there—the available one for them to dump on. In turn they learned how to work, and many times our conversations were turned in spiritual directions.

Women, we are the remodelers, the harmonizers of our homes. We are a country of broken homes, broken hearts, and broken health. Staying married today is more of a challenge than getting married. To keep the flame of love alive takes creative work. Several things need to happen.

- We need to surrender our egos to the needs of the other person. Ephesians 5:21 NIV says, "Submit to one another out of reverence for Christ."

- We need to pay attention to the other person. Make your husband feel special and unique, honoring and treating him as you would want to be treated.

- We need to see our man as our leader and hero. When you married him you saw his many fine qualities. Now be willing to follow his leadership in spite of the fact that you may be smarter, stronger, greater, prettier, wiser, and even more organized.

- We need to make our husband feel good about himself: to build him up in his eyes, our eyes, and the eyes of the world. We have the opportunity to make our husband look and feel good. Building up our hero's masculinity in his eyes and in the eyes of other people is very important.

- We need to shower our man with love. Let's not waste time arguing day and night. A smart woman will love, love, love. It takes years to learn patience, to bite your tongue and overlook faults. My Bob may not always be easy to love, but he is sure worth it. So who is the winner? We women are! We keep the harmony for us and for our children, and we preserve our love. We are the women who make or break the home.

The brokenness of our lives and homes can be repaired if we are willing. Great women are willing to make positive changes, and those changes first come in our relationship with God.

- *Submit to Him.* Give God your family, yourself, and your failures. We will never change our mate or other people, but God can, and He does.

- *Commit to Him.* Give God your attitudes, your behavior, your stresses, your work, your career, and all the areas in which you feel the need for peace.

Receive or rededicate yourself to Christ. Be an active part of the family of God, and then wait to allow God to work in your family.

> *Father God, thank You for choosing me to be the heart of our home. By nature that is my love. I get so excited when I see how my family responds to all that I do. Yes, there are times when I have to ask for a thank you, but thank You for giving me a husband, children, and grandchildren who respond in such a positive fashion when I do my mother things. I know I have made a positive impact when I see my children, Jenny and Brad, do some of the same things in their homes. May those reading today's thoughts step out in a new way. Amen.*

Taking Action

- ❧ Submit to God in this area of your life.

- ❧ Commit to God your attitudes and behavior in this area.

- ❧ Set the thermostat in your home by having a candle and flowers on tonight's dinner table (do it even if only you show up).

- Have soft music playing while eating (no television or loud noises allowed).

- Write your husband and children love notes and put them on their pillows.

Reading On

Proverbs 14:1	Deuteronomy 6:5
1 Corinthians 3:12,13	John 13:35

WE ARE LIBERATED

- Liberated in our homes because we've built a strong foundation.

- Liberated in our lives as we live a life built with strong bricks.

- Liberated in our professions because we are creative women and can have a balance between home, work, family, and church.

- Liberated in traditionalism as we learn from the mistakes of the past and move toward the future with excitement and less stress.

- Liberated in Jesus Christ because He is our source of strength, love, forgiveness, peace, and joy.

A God of Order

Scripture Reading: Colossians 4:1-6

Key Verse: Colossians 4:5

Conduct yourselves with wisdom toward outsiders, making the most of the opportunity.

In Scripture we find that the concept of organization and order deals far more with our *relationships with people* than with our *handling of things*. When we do things in order, we find ourselves moving through life with purpose and meaning. God delights in turning weaknesses into strengths and in bringing order from confusion (1 Corinthians 14:10). He redeems our time as well as our toils (Colossians 4:5).

When we are in order, we find that we have smoother communication, more effective problem-solving, better task management, better interpersonal relationships, and better direction of what needs to be done.

There are several places in Scripture where God directed order.

- Moses was to establish a multitiered judicial system (Exodus 18:13-26).

- Jesus directed the hungry masses to be seated on the grass so they could be fed (Mark 6:39,40).

- Jesus sent His disciples out two by two and gave them specific guidelines (Mark 6:7).

Scripture wants us to be organized so that our lives will be lived without chaos and confusion and that we will have maximum freedom for achieving His goals in our lives.

Over the years I have received countless letters from women who want to know how to get organized. Perhaps through coaxing from their husbands, children, friends, or clergy, they have begun to realize that they could be more effective if they could somehow get organized.

The word organized means many things to many people. For some it might mean putting their papers in colored file folders, for some it means putting all their seasonings in ABC order, for some it means a clean house, and for others it means being able to retrieve papers that have been stored away.

Even after writing books with a combined total of over 4600 pages and over a million copies in print dealing with the single topic of organization, I'm not sure I have covered all bases for all women. However, I have found the following to be basic requirements when a person wants to become organized.

- *Start with you.* What is it about you that causes you to be disorganized? I find that organized people have a calmness and serenity about them that disorganized people don't have. Search your own self to see what is causing all that confusion. See if you can't get rid of that clutter before you move on. In some cases you may need to meet with your clergy or even a professional counselor who can help you unravel the causes of this disorganization. (I didn't say it was going to be easy to get organized!)

- *Keep it simple.* There are many programs available, but choose one that's simple. You don't want to spend all your time keeping up charts and graphs.

- *Make sure everything has a designated place.* One of our sayings is "Don't put it down, put it away."

Another is "Don't pile it, file it." If there is no place for stuff to go, it's going to get piled. That's one thing you want to prevent—piles.

- *Store like items together.* Bob has his gardening supplies and tools together. I have my laundry items in one place, my bill-paying tools in one area, my prayer basket and its tools together, my cups/saucers, my drinking glasses, and my dinnerware all in their general area. You don't want to spend time going from here to there getting ready for your tasks. Put like things in one place.

- *Even though you are neat, you may not be organized.* I tell my women to use notebook organizers and that there are two things they need to remember: One, write it down; and two, read it. It doesn't do you much good if you write down that birthday date or that appointment on your calendar and yet you forget both because you didn't read it on the calendar. Remember to write and read.

- *Get rid of all items you don't use.* See my *More Hours in My Day* book to help you in this area. It will give you great help in getting rid of all the unused stuff.

- *Invest in the proper tools.* In order to be organized you need proper tools: bins, hooks, racks, containers, lazy Susans, etc.

- *Involve the whole family.* Learn to delegate jobs and responsibilities to other members of the family. My Bob takes care of all the repairs. When something is broken, he is Mr. Fix-It. Depending upon the ages of the children, you will need to tailor-make their chores. Also, change off frequently so they don't get bored. Don't do something yourself that another member of the family can do.

- *Keep master lists.* I've learned to use my three-ring organizer, my three-by-five file cards, and my journals to keep track of all our stuff. Many of these techniques are woven throughout my various books. You may think you'll never forget that you loaned that CD to Brad or that video to Christine, but you will. Write it down and keep the list in a place where you cannot overlook it. (In *Survival for Busy Women* I have some charts on how to do this.)

- *Continually reevaluate your system.* Nothing is written in concrete; it can be changed. See how other people do things, read a book to gather ideas, and evaluate your own system. Change it when it's not working.

- *Use a lot of labels and signs.* If containers, bins, drawers, and shelves aren't labeled, the family won't be able to spot where things go. I have also used color coding to help identify items belonging to various members of the family: blue for Bevan, red for Chad, and purple for Christine. I use a finepoint paint pen very effectively to label clothes, glass and plastic jars, and wooden items. (Don't use water-base pens—they will not last very long.) You can also purchase a label maker for around six dollars at a variety store.

Where to start? Start with these suggestions. Get them under control, and then you can move into more specific areas.

Remember that the end result is to give you more available time to do God's will for your life. People always matter more to the Lord than rules.

> *Father God, I thank You for being a God of order. Your examples have been a great inspiration for my life. I appreciate how you take confusion and chaos and make it meaningful. My life has certainly been a living example of that. May my readers see Your model and know that order can be learned and is not just something we are born with.*
>
> *I certainly like the extra time You give me so I can give You more time doing the ministry You have for me. Amen.*

Taking Action

☙ Think on these thoughts: Why are you disorganized? Is there something about your life that is causing chaos? Examine yourself and see what needs to be done internally first.

☙ Go to your hall closet, if you have one, and clean it out. Reorganize the contents, and discard or give away what you are no longer using.

Reading On

Ephesians 5:15,16 Matthew 15:35
Exodus 18:13-26   Mark 6:7

People before things; people before projects; family before friends; husband before children; husband before parents; tithe before wants; Bible before opinions; Jesus before all.

❑ ❑ ❑

Mary, Martha, Me

Scripture Reading: Luke 10:38-42

Key Verse: Luke 10:42

Mary has chosen the good part, which shall not be taken away from her.

This truly is the dilemma of today's woman. I've been more like Martha than like Mary. I desire to be like Mary, but my Martha side keeps getting in the way. Is Mary the better woman? For the moment she probably had more focus on the priorities that needed immediate attention. As Jesus entered Bethany from a hectic teaching schedule He just wanted to kick back and do the real basics. He didn't want a big party with a lot of people continuing to draw His energy. He had just had a big day and He only wanted a basic meal with the opportunity to get to bed early and have a good night's rest.

I can really relate to that situation. Often after I have given a Friday evening and Saturday seminar a very gracious person on the sponsoring committee wants to have a party in my honor. I deeply appreciate that and will go and be upbeat, courteous, and cheerful, but often I would just as soon take off my dress clothes and shoes, throw myself on the bed of the hotel, and REST. I'm sure that's how Jesus felt on this occasion.

My *Martha side* says I've been waiting for this special guest in my home and I want it to be clean and in order. I'm sure she swept, mopped, scoured, dusted, and cleaned all day. She probably did the dishes, the laundry, the ironing, the dusting, and the cooking. Of course there was the mending and the feeding of the children too. She had worked so hard to make everything just right, but now she felt abandoned because Mary, who was to help her, left her side and just sat at Jesus' feet. Martha needed help to carry this party off, but Mary was giving her no help. So Martha became a little impatient.

My Mary side says housework can wait; Jesus is more important. He doesn't come this way very often, and I need to spend my time with His needs. I can always tidy up after He journeys on His way.

Martha/Mary/me says I need a balance in my tidiness and in my passion for other people's needs. Discernment is very important as we try to prioritize our activities. In fact Martha got so upset with Mary that she went to Jesus for help. She asked, "Lord, do You not care that my sister has left me to do all the serving alone? Then tell her to help me." I'm sure Martha was disappointed with Jesus' reply: "Martha, Martha, you are worried and bothered about so many things; but only a few things are necessary, really only one, for Mary has chosen the good part, which shall not be taken away from her."

Jesus said that Mary was pleasing Him by paying attention to Him and His situation. It wasn't that Martha's activity wasn't useful, but for the moment the "being" of Mary was better than the "doing" of Martha. The Martha of me nags to keep my house in order each day, but my Mary side says gently, "I need time to pray." Martha is concerned with what neighbors might think if they drop in and find dishes stacked in the kitchen sink. But Mary answers, "Selfish! I think it's a crime if you don't share with others your talents and time."

Both issues must be addressed in our lives. For us to move effectively as wife, mom, and maybe outside employee, we must learn to say no to good things and save our yes for the very best. We have to balance out the Martha and Mary sides of our lives so that our Lord is pleased with what we do. If we don't take charge of our own lives, someone else will.

Father God, again Scripture has put before me the options of life. Let me be so discerning that I will know when to act properly. I don't want to clean when I need to take care of personal needs around me. On the other hand I don't want to be so casual in ministry that I don't recognize the basic needs of my home and family. Let me balance these out in my life so I can be more effective in serving You. Amen.

Taking Action

 When do you need to be more like Martha?

 When do you need to be more like Mary?

 How will you balance out the two?

 Send a card to a needy friend today.

 Clean out the silverware drawer.

Reading On

Matthew 20:28	John 12:26
Galatians 5:13	Romans 12:11

A man should be encouraged
to do what the Maker of him
has intended by the making of
him, according as the gifts have
been bestowed on him for that
purpose.

—*Thomas Carlyle*

A Yarmelke Christmas

Scripture Reading: John 8:12-20

Key Verse: John 8:12

I am the light of the world; he who follows Me shall not walk in the darkness, but shall have the light of life.

Finding a happy way to celebrate Christmas with my side of the family has always been difficult. Trying to bond the Jewish side with the Christian beliefs just didn't happen easily. So over the years when the families came to our homes, we would have a country Christmas with a decorated tree, garlands, twinkly lights, angels, and lots of packages. As the years went on, I became braver and braver in incorporating some Christian traditions: tucking Scripture verses under the coffee and tea cups, reading a Christmas story, and even singing Christmas carols. My Jewish family endured these Christian Christmas events over the years.

In 1982 I began to give holiday seminars, which included organizing for Thanksgiving and Christmas, gift giving, gift wrapping, building memories, Christ-centered traditions, and ending the three hours with a "festival of lights." This part is where I tell the story of Hanukkah and describe how it is celebrated in Jewish homes all over the world. I light the menorah candles as the story is told. When all my candles are lit, the room sparkles with the beauty of the candles shining. The lights look like twinkling stars.

But it doesn't end there. As I continue, everyone is still looking at the menorah and its beauty. If we look and watch long enough, the candles eventually burn down, blow out, or spark out. But when we have the light of the Messiah in our hearts the light never goes out.

After eight years of 23 seminars in 45 days, my own light went on as to our own personal family Christmas. Why hadn't I thought of it sooner? So my new plan went into action. I couldn't wait for December to come that year. I sent invitations to all the family as usual, and as usual they all showed up, even my Uncle Hyman's cousin from New York. That year Hanukkah came during our family event date, which was perfect for my new plan. The menorah was on the table and the candles were ready to be lit. As usual, I had the Scripture verses tucked under the cups, with a story ready to be read and songs ready to be sung.

My family, right off, saw the menorah displayed, much to their surprise. We then asked my Uncle Hy to be the acting rabbi for the family and to tell the Hanukkah story and light the candles. A serious smile came over his face and a twinkle lit up his eyes. Yarmelkes were passed out to all the men and even the small young boys. (A yarmelke is a small black cap that is worn only on the crown part of a male's head as a sign of reverence to God.) It was a special sight. My uncle took his job seriously and the short service began. We all stood around him, and the menorah candles began to sparkle their lights throughout the living room. It was wonderful. We then proceeded into the living room for a great traditional turkey meal.

That event totally changed the attitude of my family, and we were praised for a beautiful party and a yarmelke Christmas, tying the two faiths together.

It was the best Christmas ever, and thus began a new tradition in our family.

In our key verse today, Jesus draws an analogy between the sun as the physical light of the world and Himself as the spiritual light of the world. This theme is also mentioned in the ninth chapter of John.

In my own Christian walk, I have found that the light that permeates from Jesus and His Scriptures has given me direction when the way seems dark. Often darkness gives dark advice, so we have to go to a light source to illuminate the truth.

Light is always a threat to darkness. If we go into a gathering where there is darkness and turn on a light, the people gathered there will shout, "Please turn down the lights!" Darkness doesn't like light because it exposes evil deeds.

Father God, help me to remember the needs of those in my family who come from other faiths. May Your spirit be present in times together and open the hearts of those who do not know You personally. It is because of You, Lord, that we can love one another, for Your light gives truth. Amen.

Taking Action

 Write a note to a family member and tell him or her one reason why you love him.

 Plan ways you can let the light of the Lord shine in your life. What will you specifically do?

 Smile and laugh more.

Reading On

John 9:5   Genesis 1:3
John 11:9,10   Psalm 27:1

In darkness there is no choice. It is light that enables us to see the difference between things; and it is Christ who gives us light.

—C.T. Whitmell

What Is Love?

Scripture Reading: 1 Corinthians 13:4-8

Key Verse: 1 Corinthians 13:4-8
Read the complete passage.

One of the most searching questions we have to answer as adults is, "What is love?" We see people who search so hard yet seem to miss the mark and aren't able to grasp love in either their heads or their hearts.

The people of the nineties seem so dysfunctional when it comes to this topic of love. In our reading, hearing, and expounding we seem to miss the mark of what is truly love. As young babies we enter the world with all kinds of love bestowed on us by our parents and grandparents. They make such a fuss over us and give us so much attention, but then we seem to lose grasp of this concept. In most cases they have decided to love us no matter what. Yet, somehow through the years we go from a *decision* to love to a *feeling* of love.

Our modern culture has gone from decision to feeling in a matter of just a few years. From looking around we see that loving and being loved are not as easy as we would like to think.

What started out as mother's love has declined to the point of dysfunction in the current family. We have lost our focus on true love. Some of the confusing signals we get when thinking about love include:

- Falling in and out of love
- A feeling too deep for words

- Never having to say you're sorry
- We'll give it a trial run
- A sickness full of woes
- A warm puppy.

No wonder we're confused when we get serious about true love!

The Greeks understood three levels of love:

- Agape: love for an adorable object
- Eros : physical love between husband and wife
- Phileo: brotherly love for others.

The Western culture tries to describe these relationships by one encompassing word "love." We use a confusing word that doesn't let us define degrees or types of love.

This agape love that is found today in our readings characterizes God (1 John 4:8) and what He manifested in the gift of His Son (John 3:16). It is more than mutual affection; it expresses unselfish esteem of the object loved. Christ's love for us is undeserved and without thought of return. It was and is a decision, not a fuzzy feeling.

> Deeper love . . . down to our
> very soul. It's there we have an
> anchor who will not let us go;
> the Lord who calmed the sea is
> the One who sees us through;
> He's given us a deeper love.
>
> —*Diane Machen*

Our son Brad and his wife, Maria, used this passage in 1 Corinthians at their wedding. This portion of Scripture is used more than any other when two people want to consummate their love in marriage. Unfortunately, many times it is used as good verse and literature, but only lip service is given to the message.

As Paul wrote to the church in Corinth he told them to come together in love rather than chaos and disharmony. He contrasted the present with what Christ would be like in heaven as he showed the supremacy of love over the conflicts of gifts. He began:

> Love is patient, love is kind and is not jealous;
> Love does not brag and is not arrogant,
> Love does not act unbecomingly;
> It does not seek its own, is not provoked,
> Does not take into account a wrong suffered,
> Does not rejoice in unrighteousness,
> But rejoices with the truth;
> Bears all things, hopes all things, endures all things.
> Love never fails.

If we could only recapture this agape love that Paul spoke about, we could become healthy, wholesome, and functional families again. My cry is that love is much more than a warm puppy. It is an act of an unselfish decision to love and honor your commitment made at the altar between husband, wife, and God.

> *Father God, I appreciate Your sharing with me again what love is all about. I sometimes get so confused between decision and feeling. I'm continually bombarded with this concept of feeling good. Truly every day I must willfully decide again to love my mate. Don't ever let me get distracted and become conformed to the world. I want to be transformed by the renewing of my mind. Thank You for giving me a good marriage with a love that encompasses agape, eros, and phileo. Amen.*

Taking Action

- ❦ In your journal list from today's passage what true love is.

- ❦ In what areas of your life has feeling taken over decision?

❦ What are you going to do about it?

❦ Tell your mate these words today:

> "I believe in you."

> "I want you."

> "You're the greatest."

Reading On

Romans 12:2	1 John 4:8
John 3:16	Deuteronomy 6:5

> When iron is rubbed against a magnet it becomes magnetic. Just so, love is caught, not taught. One heart burning with love sets another on fire. The church was built on love; it proves what love can do.
>
> —*Frank C. Laubach*

If You Are Only Kind

Scripture Reading: Ephesians 4:25-32

Key Verse: Ephesians 4:32

> *Be kind to one another, tenderhearted, forgiving each other, just as God in Christ also has forgiven you.*

———— ❦ ————

As a society we have forgotten to teach this very important element of character called kindness. Of course our media doesn't see kindness because that doesn't spark reader and advertising interest. People have become almost immune to the truly good things of life. If a movie doesn't have the most thrilling special effects it won't have people flocking to the box office to pay for the tremendous budgets of producing films today.

Even our literature and songs must have violence and exposé in order to attract attention. Even our schools have left out the teaching of character. Our students have a very difficult time learning about values, and when they do, the question arises, "Whose and what?" Going to biblical principles is prohibited because of confusion on the subject of "church and state." Therefore it is up to our homes and churches to teach about kindness. As parents we have to have a specific desire to teach such values.

We can go to our Christian bookstore and ask for referrals on books, videos, and music that have a message of values. The modern Christian bookstore is a tremendous resource on such topics.

Ways that Bob and I have found to be effective in teaching good values include:

- reading good literature to the children on a regular basis;

- modeling good character traits in the home;

- listening to wholesome music;

- not watching television very often and restricting certain sitcoms that are downers;

- making sure the children are involved in good youth organizations that teach values;

- having the children be involved around strong models who exhibit like values;

- encouraging strong, outside-the-immediate-family support from Sunday school teachers, coaches, aunts, uncles, and grandparents;

- having family conference times where values can be discussed.

Throughout the life of Christ He exhibited various acts of kindness in how He responded to situations, people, and things.

In our key verse today we see commands that deal with this subject:

- Be kind to one another.

- Be tenderhearted.

- Be forgiving to each other.

Why? Because "God in Christ also has forgiven you." The basis for us as believers forgiving others lies in the fact that we ourselves have been graciously forgiven by God and released from any obligation to make restitution. This concept of understanding what Jesus did for us on the cross is the basis of our kindness to others. We as humans can't forgive unless we understand forgiveness as modeled by God in Christ.

As parents we often spend more time in teaching our children how to be dancers, actors, musicians, athletes, and scholars than in teaching them character values. As a country we need young people who have true strength of character. I challenge you today to think of how you are going to teach your children kindness.

> *Father God, I thank You for forgiving me of my sins. Only by Your grace can I be freed from the imprisonment of unforgiven sin. On the cross Christ paid for all my past, present, and future sins. Because You have forgiven me I am able now to forgive others. Because of this forgiveness, I am able to relate to others with kindness, tenderheartedness, and forgiveness. May I always be true to Your will for my life, and may others see Christ in me. Amen.*

Taking Action

❧ Thank God for your forgiveness as a believer.

❧ If you aren't a believer you may want to investigate the life of Christ and see if you can accept who He was and is.

❧ Develop a plan with your spouse (if you have one) on how you are going to teach values to your children.

Reading On

Proverbs 19:22   2 Corinthians 6:6
Galatians 5:22,23   2 Peter 1:7

MARY'S LAMB

Mary had a little lamb,
Its fleece was white as snow;
And everywhere that Mary went,
The lamb was sure to go.

He followed her to school one day,
Which was against the rule;
It made the children laugh and play,
To see a lamb at school.

And so the teacher turned him out,
But still he lingered near,
And waited patiently about,
Till Mary did appear.

Then he ran to her, and laid
His head upon her arm,
As if he said, "I'm not afraid—
You'll keep me from all harm."

"What makes the lamb love Mary so?"
The eager children cried.
"Oh, Mary loves the lamb, you know,"
The teacher quick replied.

And you each gentle animal
In confidence may bind,
And make them follow at your will,
If you are only kind.

—*Sarah Josepha Hale*

❏ ❏ ❏

Planning Your Days

Scripture Reading: Matthew 6:25-34

Key Verse: Matthew 6:33

> *Seek first His kingdom and His righteousness, and all these things shall be added to you.*

We live in a very anxious society. Many of us are more worried about tomorrow than today. We bypass all of today's contentment because of our worry about what might happen tomorrow. In our passage today we read that the early Christians asked the same basic questions (verse 31):

- What shall we eat?
- What shall we drink?
- With what shall we clothe ourselves?

Jesus tells them in verse 34, "Do not be anxious for tomorrow, for tomorrow will care for itself. Each day has enough trouble of its own." Then He gives them a formula for establishing the right priorities of life in verse 33: "Seek first His kingdom and His righteousness, and all these things shall be added to you." My Bob and I have used this verse as our mission verse for the last 35 years. Each day we claim these two instructions:

- Seek His kingdom.
- Seek His righteousness.

When we seek these two things we find that our day takes shape and we can say "yes" we will do that or "no" we will not do that. Often we are overwhelmed by having too many things to do. Life offers many good choices on how to schedule our time. But we all have only 24 hours a day. How are we to use those hours effectively?

When we begin to set priorities, we determine what is important and what isn't, and how much time we are willing to give each activity.

The Bible gives us guidelines for the godly ordering of our lives:

- Our personal relationship to Him (Matthew 6:33; Philippians 3:8).

- Our time for home and family (Genesis 2:24; Psalm 127:3; 1 Timothy 3:2-5).

- Our time for work (1 Thessalonians 4:11,12).

- Our time for ministry and community activities (Colossians 3:17).

We cannot do all the things that come our way. My Bob and I have a saying that helps us when we have too many choices: "Say no to the good things and save each yes for the best."

Don't be afraid to say no. If you have established Matthew 6:33 as one of the key verses in your life you can very quickly decide whether a particular opportunity will help you to—

- seek God's kingdom;

- seek God's righteousness.

After learning to say no easily, you can begin to major on the big things of life and not get bogged down with issues that don't really matter.

Father God, since You are a God of order I also want to have order in my life. Thank You for sharing this verse with our family many years ago. It has certainly helped us to major on the major and minor on the minor issues of life. May other women get excited about not being anxious for tomorrow and realize that You take care of our daily needs. Amen.

Taking Action

- 🍂 Look in the mirror and say no 10 times. Do this every day for a week.

- 🍂 Memorize Matthew 6:33 and write it in your journal.

- 🍂 Each morning write out a "to-do list." After each activity write yes or no. Then disregard each no.

- 🍂 Rank each yes in order of importance. (Let the most important one be number 1.)

- 🍂 Cross off each activity as you get it accomplished.

Reading On

Psalm 119:105   1 Corinthians 14:40
Psalm 32:8   Luke 5:15,16

Do all the good you can, By all
the means you can, In all the
ways you can, In all the places
you can, At all the times you
can, To all the people you can,
As long as ever you can.

—*John Wesley*

The Blankie

Scripture Reading: John 14:27-31

Key Verse: John 14:27

> *Peace I leave with you; My peace I give to you. Not as the world gives do I give to you. Let not your heart be troubled, nor let it be fearful.*

When our first grandchild was born, her parents named her Christine Marie. Christine from her mother's middle name and Marie from my middle name. As a namesake I'm very proud of Christine Marie. At this writing she is our only grand-daughter, along with four grandsons. We love them too!

From flannel fabric I made her a piece of pink-printed blanket with some small roses. The blanket was edged with a pink satin binding. It was only about 8 inches square. Well, as you might guess, it became her security blankie while she sucked her thumb. The blankie got twisted, wadded up, and smoothed by little Christine. She was finally able to pull loose an end and twist the threads around her fingers.

Christine loved her pink rosebud blankie. It gave her comfort when she was hurt, softness when she was afraid, and security when she felt alone. Then one day five years later the blankie got folded one last time and was put in an envelope that she tucked away in her dresser drawer.

Christine was 13 recently, and from time to time she still pulls out that envelope to look at the rosebud flannel security blanket.

Jesus is like the security blanket that Christine once held close to her—only today she has almighty God our Heavenly Father, God the Son, and God the Holy Spirit to hold tight to.

As our Scripture states, Jesus is who gives us peace in the midst of the storms of life: when we are going through that difficult tornado of a broken marriage, the death of a dream, financial troubles, childless pain, ill health, or all the other trials we encounter in just living out our daily lives.

Christ is our security blanket when we are afraid and feel fearful of tomorrow. My mama used to tell me in the middle of the night when I needed to go to the bathroom but was afraid of the dark, "Be afraid, but go." Today I know I can go because I have my Lord, who is with me wherever I go. When I'm weak and upset, He holds me and comforts my heart.

Jesus is much more than a security blanket. He is our Comforter, our Savior, the Messiah, the Alpha and Omega, the Almighty, our bright and morning star, our counselor, our strength, our redeemer, our peace, our high priest, our foundation, and our master builder.

First Corinthians 3:11 says, "No man can lay a foundation other than the one which is laid, which is Jesus Christ."

It's time to give our blanket over to Jesus and allow Him to be our Master Comforter.

Christine's blankie is now in a beautiful frame, hanging on the wall in her bedroom as a treasured memory of her babyhood. She will carry this along her lifetime from babyhood into her golden years. But best of all, she will carry Jesus in her heart for eternity.

> *Father God, thank You for letting me put away my old childhood security blanket and giving me the faith to trust You in all situations. May I never go back to my blankie. You have been so faithful to me during these adult years. You are all I need—nothing else. Amen.*

Taking Action

- List all the security blankets in your life.
- Recall a childhood memory and write it in your journal.
- Write down a time when God comforted you in difficult times. Thank Him again for that comfort.
- Praise God today for who He is, the Almighty God.

Reading On

Psalm 4:5	Isaiah 26:4
Proverbs 3:5	Hebrews 2:13

When I was a child, I used to speak as a child, think as a child, reason as a child. When I became a man, I did away with childish things.

—*1 Corinthians 13:11*

You Are Not Alone

Scripture Reading: Matthew 6:1-13

Key Verse: Matthew 6:9-13 (The Lord's Prayer)
Read the Lord's Prayer.

Some of you may not have a prayer life at all. Others of you may have a very vital prayer life. Some of you want to have a prayer life but are fumbling with it because you don't know how to incorporate it into your life or how to organize it. I was once in that position. I was fumbling in my prayer life because I didn't know the steps to take. One of my first learnings was to trust God for my every care. Often in life I had been disappointed by those I trusted, but the following helped me realize I was never alone.

ONE SET OF FOOTPRINTS

One night a man had a dream. In his dream he was walking along the beach with the Lord, when across the sky flashed all the events of his life. However, for each scene he noticed two sets of footprints in the sand, one belonging to him and the other to the Lord. When the last scene had flashed before him, he looked back at the footprints and noticed that many times along the path there was only one set of footprints in the sand. He also noticed that this happened during the lowest and saddest times of his life.

This really bothered him, so he said to the Lord, "You promised that once I decided to follow You, You would walk with me all the way, but I noticed that during the roughest times of my life there was only one set of footprints. I don't understand why You deserted me when I needed You the most."

The Lord replied, "My precious child, I love you and I would never leave you. During those times of trial and suffering when you saw only one set of footprints, it was then that I carried you."

—Author Unknown

You see, God is always with us. When the times are the lowest, that's when He picks us up and carries us. Isn't that wonderful! Some of us right now are in a position where we're being carried through a rough situation or problem in our life. It's wonderful to know that we have our Lord there to carry us when times get low and things get rough.

Often we don't take the necessary time with our Lord in prayer and communication. But do you know what? He loves us anyway. He loves us unconditionally. Prayer doesn't have to be long, either. Sometimes we get turned off because we feel it takes so much time, but it doesn't have to be long.

In several of my books I have given you a way in which you can organize your daily prayer life so you aren't overwhelmed with this phase of your spiritual life. Please refer to those chapters which give you a step-by-step plan for an organized prayer life. As I introduce ladies to prayer who aren't accustomed to a disciplined life of prayer, I want them first to be exposed to the model prayer as found in today's readings. The Lord's Prayer—

- begins with adoration of God (verse 9);
- acknowledges subjection to His will (verse 10);
- asks petitions of Him (verses 11-13a);
- ends with praise (verse 13b).

To better understand this prayer, we break it down into small phrases with their meanings. This gives us a model for all our prayers.

- "Our Father who art in heaven" (verse 9a). Recognize who He is—the Person of God.

- "Hallowed be Thy name" (verse 9b). Worship God because of who He is.

- "Thy kingdom come. Thy will be done" (verse 10). Seek and do God's will. His Word is the way to find His will.

- "Give us this day our daily bread" (verse 11). Ask God to meet your everyday needs in order to perform your godly work.

- "And forgive us our debts" (verse 12). Ask God for pardon and forgiveness in your daily failures.

- "And do not lead us into temptation" (verse 13). Ask for protection from the evils of temptation.

- "For Thine is the kingdom and the power and the glory" (verse 13). Praise God for who He is.

Father God, I so appreciate the Lord's Prayer. So many times in life I am able to recite it in moments of need and praise. I thank You for being my heavenly Father. Since my earthly father lacked some parenting skills that a young daughter needed, I find You a great support and encouragement for me in time of need. With You I find I am never alone. Amen.

Taking Action

- ❧ Memorize this model prayer.
- ❧ Recite it every night for a week before going to sleep.
- ❧ Write it down in your journal.
- ❧ Thank God for being your Father.

Reading On

Romans 8:15	1 John 5:14
Psalm 18:3	Philippians 4:9

---❧---

The true test of walking in the Spirit will not be the way we act but the way we react to the daily frustrations of life.

—*Beverly LaHaye*

---❧---

The Mitt

Scripture Reading: Isaiah 58:1-11

Key Verse: Isaiah 58:11a

The Lord will continually guide you.

It was our son Brad's first real leather baseball mitt. His dad taught him how to break it in with special break-in oil. The oil was rubbed into the pocket of the glove, then Brad tossed his baseball from hand to hand to form a pocket just right for him. Brad loved his mitt and worked for hours each day to make a comfortable mitt just for him. He was so happy to have such a special glove at his baseball practices and games.

One afternoon after practice one of the older boys asked to see Brad's mitt. He looked it over and then threw it into the grassy field. Brad ran to find his special possession, but he couldn't find it. Nowhere was his mitt to be found. With a frightened and hurt heart, Brad came home in tears with no mitt.

After he told me the story I encouraged him that it had to be there somewhere. "I'll go with you, Brad, and we'll search the lot until we find it." "But, Mom, I did search the lot and it's not there," replied Brad tearfully. So I said, "Brad, let's pray and ask God to help us." By now it was beginning to get dark and we needed to hurry, so into the car we jumped. As I drove Brad to the baseball field we asked God to guide our steps directly to the glove. Parking quickly, we both headed for the field. As I held Brad's hand we asked God to put us in the right direction.

Immediately Brad released my hand and ran into the tall grass of the field—and there about 20 feet away was Brad's glove.

Brad is a grown man today, with sons of his own. May he never forget that God always answers our prayers. Sometimes the answer is wait, yes, or later. For Brad and me, that day it was yes: "I'll direct you to find the mitt of a young boy whose heart is broken because of a bully kid and a lost glove."

> I know Christ dwells wihin me
> all the time, guiding me and in-
> spiring me whenever I do or say
> anything. A light of which I
> caught no glimmer before
> comes to me at the very mo-
> ment when it is needed.
>
> —*Saint Therese of Lisieux*

Do you have a "lost glove" today? Go before God and pray Isaiah 58:11a. If God says it, we need to believe it. He *will* direct you and guide you. Open your heart to hear His direction, and then press ahead. The grass may seem too tall for you to see very far, but trust the Lord and keep walking until you feel the peace that the found mitt will give you. God may lead in a direction that we least expect, but if we don't step forward in His direction, how will we ever know if the lost mitt will be there?

> *Father God, help me today to trust Your Word. Help me to walk in the field of grass as You continually guide me. Most of all, help me to trust You even when I don't feel like trusting because I just can't seem to find the mitt. Thank You, Lord, that You do care for a little boy's lost glove. Thank You for the peace in my heart as I hold Your hand of direction. Amen.*

Taking Action

- ❧ Thank God today for five things in your life.

- ❧ Call a friend in need and pray with her by phone.

- ❧ Thank God that He is in control and that He will lead you to the answer of your prayers.

Reading On

Proverbs 15:8   Matthew 18:19,20
1 Thessalonians 5:17   Romans 8:35

I have been driven many times to my knees by the overwhelming conviction that I had nowhere else to go.

—*Abraham Lincoln*

A Mark of Distinction

Scripture Reading: 2 Samuel 14:25,26

Key Verse: 2 Samuel 14:26

When he cut the hair of his head . . . he weighed the hair of his head at 200 shekels.

———— ❧ ————

All throughout history, hair has been a mark of distinction. The length, color, and style have been focal points in all societies. When our children were in junior high and high school our heated discussions were related to hair fashion.

Even today as I read popular magazines I see striking advertising relating to hair care. My Bob always tells me that I and most women friends of ours think the next new hairstylist will be the one who recaptures our youth with the perfect hairstyle. It is true that most of us are looking for the hair designer who will cut, tone, and color our hair the best. Shampoos and rinses are also popular searches for us. We realize that hair and its proper care mean a lot to the American culture.

In the Old Testament, Absalom had beautiful hair that was admired by many. Today's verse states that he weighed his hair and found it to be 200 shekels, or about three or four pounds in our measurement. That's a lot of hair!

Length of hair in the New Testament was considered a mark of distinction between men and women (1 Corinthians 11:14,15). A woman's long hair is given to her for a covering. Hair represents the proper covering in the natural realm, even as the veil is the proper covering in the religious realm.

The veil of the temple was the heavily woven curtain that hung between the Holy Place and the Most Holy Place (Luke 23:45; Hebrews 9:3). Its presence was a continual reminder of the separation between mankind and God. The writer of Hebrews states that the veil represented Jesus' body (Hebrews 10:19,20). The tearing of the veil at Jesus' death on the cross signified the removal of the barrier between God and anyone who would accept Jesus' sacrifice (Hebrews 4:16; 6:19).

Scripture addresses several areas relating to hair:

- Excessive adornment of hair (1 Timothy 2:9; 1 Peter 3:3).
- Wisdom and experience of those with gray hair (1 Samuel 12:2; Job 15:10).
- Ointment for hair as a mark of hospitality (Luke 7:46).

We have also worked hair-related phrases from Scripture into our culture:

- "Not one hair of his head [shall] fall to the ground" (1 Samuel 14:45).
- "More numerous than the hairs of my head" (Psalm 40:12).
- "The very hairs of your head are all numbered" (Matthew 10:30).

What we take as everyday fashion sometimes has tremendous religious significance and origination. Our hair truly is a mark of distinction that needs to be respected as God's gift to us. First Peter 3:3,4 says, "Let not your adornment be merely external—braiding the hair; and wearing gold jewelry, or putting on dresses; but let it be the hidden person of the heart, with the imperishable quality of a gentle and quiet spirit, which is precious in the sight of God."

Father God, I truly want to have the heart that reflects the quality of a gentle and quiet spirit. Each day I yearn to be acceptable in Your sight by my speech, attitude, selection of clothes, and outward adornment. I want to be sensitive in these areas so I'm not offensive to another brother or sister in Christ. Don't let me get mired down in worldly fashions that send out the wrong signals to those around me. Amen.

Taking Action

- Evaluate your external adornment. Would it be precious in the sight of God?

- List the areas that wouldn't glorify God. What changes need to be made?

- How is your gentle and quiet spirit doing?

- What changes need to be made in this area?

Reading On

1 Corinthians 11:14,15   Hebrews 10:19,20
1 Peter 3:3,4   1 Timothy 2:9

God's fingers can touch nothing
but to mold it into loveliness.

—*George MacDonald*

Like a Counterfeit $100 Bill

Scripture Reading: 1 Samuel 2:11-30

Key Verse: 1 Samuel 2:30b
Far be it from Me—for those who honor Me I will honor, and those who despise Me will be lightly esteemed.

A young man had just graduated from law school and had set up an office, proudly displaying his shingle out front. On his first day at work, as he sat at his desk with his door open, he wondered how to get his first client. Then he heard footsteps coming down the long corridor toward his office.

Not wanting this potential client to think he would be his first, he quickly picked up the telephone and began to talk loudly to a make-believe caller.

"Oh, yes sir," the young lawyer exclaimed into the phone, "I'm very experienced in corporate law. . . . Courtroom experience? Why, yes, I've had several cases."

The sound of steps drew closer to his open door.

"I have broad experience in almost every category of legal work," he continued, loud enough for his impending visitor to hear.

Finally, with the steps right at his door, he replied, "Expensive? Oh, no sir, I'm very reasonable. I'm told my rates are among the lowest in town."

The young lawyer then excused himself from his "conversation" and covered the phone to respond to the prospective client who was now standing in the doorway. With his most confident voice he said, "Yes, sir, may I help you?"

"Well, yes, you can," the man said with a smirk. "I'm the telephone repairman, and I've come to hook up your phone!"[17]

We sometimes fake the Christian life in this same way. Preoccupied with self and wanting our own way, we ignore God and pretend to be spiritual. Instead of having Christ's character imprinted on our lives, we go our own way, and our Christianity becomes a forgery. Like a counterfeit $100 bill, we may look real, but we lack genuine value.

Do we fake the Christian life ourselves? On Sunday, do we act and talk Christian, but come Monday or when we are away from church, do we forget all about our Christianity? If so, we are just like the young lawyer. We look good, we talk good, and we act good, but our communication to God isn't right.

We feel best when our heart is in good relationship to God. On the other hand, when we are disobedient to God we place a terrible yoke of guilt upon ourselves. On these occasions we feel like the counterfeit $100 bill—worthless.

Each day as we awake from our sleep we have two basic decisions to make:

- Not to obey God today.
- To obey God today.

What we choose each day will determine our course for that day and eventually for our entire life. For us to live by faith in God we have to be active in choosing what is right. True faith is not passive; it is an active process. Does this mean that if we choose to disobey God we will have a bad day and if we choose to obey God we will have a good day? I wish it were that easy, but sometimes the opposite is true.

In our Scripture for today we see how Eli's sons fell under God's disapproval because of their wrong choices in disobeying God. Eli's two sons were in the priesthood of the nation of Israel, but they were not interested in serving their father's God. First Samuel 2:12 says they were worthless men and didn't know the Lord. They were willfully disobedient and scorned God's commands. So in verse 30b God says, "Far be it from me—for those who honor me I will honor, and those who despise me will be lightly esteemed."

The one who obeys will be honored by God, but the one who disobeys will be lightly esteemed by God. As we look at those who live a life of disobedience toward God, we see dysfunctional people in today's society. Eli's family would also have been a good example of such dysfunction.

"Dysfunctional families have common patterns:

- They do not talk (keeping family secrets);
- They do not see (ignoring inappropriate behavior as well as altered perception of reality);
- They do not feel (disregarding legitimate emotions);
- They do not trust (living in isolation and fearing more broken promises).

The children strive desperately to be perfect, trying to meet all parental expectations."[18]

What our hurting country needs today is a great spiritual revival that will touch people's hearts to want to obey God. The end result will be a nation that is honored for obeying God.

You as a parent can start that revival by announcing to the world that you and your family will serve the Lord God, and that you are no longer willing to live the life of a counterfeit $100 bill. You want to be an authentic Christian.

———— 🌹 ————

Father God, I don't want to be a fake Christian. I want to be real in all aspects of my life. When my family sees me, I want them to know what a real Christian looks like. Help me to train my children to be believers of Your commandments. Thank You, Lord, for letting me hold my head up high because I know I am special in Your sight. Amen.

Taking Action

🌹 List three to five new goals to become a better model as a Christian woman.

🌹 How are you going to teach your child(ren) to be lovers of God?

🌹 What changes will you implement in your relationship with your husband?

🌹 Complete this thought in your journal: "I know God loves me because _____."

Reading On

1 Corinthians 3:16   1 Corinthians 12:1-31
Ephesians 2:10   Ruth 1:16,17

———————— 🌹 ————————

Self-discipline never means giving up anything, for giving up is a loss. Our Lord did not ask us to give up things of earth, but to exchange them for better things.

—*Fulton J. Sheen*

———————— 🌹 ————————

Hurting Hearts

Scripture Reading: Matthew 19:3-12

Key Verse: Matthew 19:6
What therefore God has joined together, let no man separate.

———— ❦ ————

Over 41 years ago my Bob and I made a commitment to God that we would live together for better or for worse, in sickness and in health. At the time it was a piece of cake to make that promise to God. We were young, naive, and very much in love. All we could think of was getting married, making a cozy home, and living happily ever after.

I wish it were as easy as that, but life brings many turns, curves, mountains, and valleys. We've experienced all the above and we've not ended the journey yet. There will be more to come as we continue on our road of marriage.

The one reason Bob and I are still celebrating anniversaries is because we both believe in commitment and the Word of God. Yes, there were times we could have bailed out when our marriage was cold or lukewarm, but we kept lighting the fire, mending the rips and tears in our relationship, and working on new and creative ways to build our marriage. We've gone to workshops, seminars, retreats, and whatever we could to build a strong wall around us to protect us from the enemy's attack. We wanted this so both our children could feel secure in a home where Mom and Dad honored and respected each other.

But formulas don't always work: The walls can crumble in spite of them. Today over 50 percent of first marriages end in divorce, and 60 percent of second marriages. The children are the ones who suffer the most; they are the true victims.

So what is the answer? It begins at the start of the marriage: the commitment made followed by a lot of hard work. Premarital counseling for six months is not too much anymore. Building a strong foundation and cleaning up the trash and baggage in our lives is critical before the "I do's" are said.

When parents of friends of ours divorced after 32 years of marriage, with five grown children and several grandchildren, they brought distress to the whole family. Yes, they had had a lot of valleys, but they also had had a lot of joys. But when a mate decides not to be married any longer, the walls fall as if hit by a major earthquake. For an adult, it seems like it wouldn't hurt when Mom and Dad divorce, but as our friends said, it's even harder because you're old enough to know all the garbage that goes with divorce.

Our typist's parents divorced when she was in her late twenties, and her world fell apart. Is it easy to be loyal to both parents in such a case? I don't think so. Usually there is a struggle to avoid taking sides. The Word of God states strongly that God hates divorce (Malachi 2:16). Yes, hearts can change, wounds can heal, God forgives, and life goes forward. But we always live with the consequences of a broken marriage, a broken home, and broken children.

God's purpose in creating man and woman (husband and wife) is for them to become "one flesh." It is a oneness of kinship or fellowship, with the physical body as the medium causing marriage to reach the deepest physical and spiritual unity. (See Genesis 2:24.)

The binding commitment of marriage does not depend upon human wills or upon what any individual does or does not do, but rather upon God's original design and purpose for marriage (Hosea 3:1-3).

God rejects divorce for several reasons:

- Marriage is a divine institution (Genesis 1:27; 2:18, 20-25).

- Marriage is by the command of the Creator (Matthew 19:4-6).

- Marriage brings two people together as one (Genesis 2:24; Matthew 19:6).

- Jesus points to the first couple (Matthew 19:8).

- Bad consequences comes with separation (Matthew 19:9).

God does hate divorce, but He also desires to work redemptively when the person who has experienced this tragedy is repentant and desires reconciliation to God.

From my own heart I know the pain. I'm watching the consequences at the time of this writing. Our daughter is in divorce proceedings after 2½ years of separation from her husband.

I've learned much through this experience. God is teaching me to trust Him, forgive others, and thank Him in all things through the name of Jesus.

I still believe in commitment and reconciliation, and I believe we have an awesome God. Today is the first day of the rest of our lives. Let's move ahead and take action.

> *Father God, help me today to take action to forgive and forget. Especially help me to look at the positive and to thank You for that. I don't want to dwell on the negative, for every day with Jesus is sweeter than the day before. Be with those who are considering breaking their marital commitment. Give them the faith and strength to live out the Scriptures. Amen.*

Taking Action

- Recommit to your original marriage commitment.

- If forgiveness is needed, go to God and ask Him to help you forgive the one who may have hurt you.

- Put the past to rest. Don't look back, but move ahead with the power of the Lord in your life.

Reading On

John 15:5   Genesis 2:24
Psalm 37:5,6   Matthew 5:32

God can do wonders with a broken heart if you give Him all the pieces.

—*Victor Alfsen*

The Bed
and Breakfast

Scripture Reading: 1 Peter 4:1-9

Key Verse: 1 Peter 4:9

*Cheerfully share your home with those who need a meal
or a place to stay for the night* (TLB).

———— ❦ ————

Over the past few years we have had the opportunity to
stay in many "bed and breakfasts" as well as some lovely inns.
Our friends Rich and Sue Gregg are continually opening their
home to missionaries, students, and anyone else who needs a
room for a short period of time (although some have stayed
longer than initially intended).

Those who come to visit and stay in our one guest room,
which we have named the "Princess Room," have commented
that we should open it as a bed and breakfast. We named our
room after our daughter, who we called "Princess" when she
was a young girl at home. We hope to give our guests the feeling of being treated as a prince or princess when they sleep in
the high bed with the down mattress and cozy bedding.

With their wake-up call is presented a tray of hot fresh
coffee, tea, a candle, flowers, toast, and a scone or some other
type of early morning beginning, all at no charge. This is all
fun and easy for me to do with a cheerful heart. However, the
Scripture for today says we should share our home "with those
who need a meal." Would I readily bring home the person
standing in the park or by the street corner who has no home?

In today's social climate one should use some discretion when hosting strangers.

Every week our church cooks a meal for the homeless in Fairmont Park. Our grandchildren have gone several times to help serve some of these meals. In downtown Los Angeles, as well as in many cities all over the country, bed and breakfasts are provided for the street people. They're not as fancy and beautiful as the ones we've stayed in, but they provide an opportunity for the homeless to shower, eat, sleep, and hear the Word of God.

All of this reminds me to be thankful for what we have. I say often in my seminars that we can always find someone who has less than we have, as well as those who have more. Let's be thankful for what we have, and make the best of that to glorify God in it.

Let's open our doors to the helpless. Let's share a meal and provide a respite in the life of a busy, stressed-out friend or even one who is just in need of some stillness in his or her life.

God says we are to have a cheerful heart in our hospitality. Let us also give another person a cheerful heart today. Regardless of how large or small a home we may have, we can share it with someone else and break bread together. Your church can help you find someone in need, or perhaps you could simply invite someone home from church for soup and bread.

"Hospitality is the practice of welcoming, sheltering, and feeding—with no thought of personal gain—those who come to our door. Much more than elegant menus, elaborate table settings, or lavish entertainment—hospitality is sharing what we have and who we are with whomever God sends. Hospitality includes setting aside time for fellowship and being flexible in order to accommodate impromptu gatherings."[19]

You can share your heart and your life with others, even if the meal is simple and the setting is humble. The most important gift of welcome simply says, "I care, I love you, and I have prepared a place for you."

> *Father God, please give me a cheerful heart for others. Help me to meet a need in someone's life who has less than I do. Thank You for those who share a ministry to the homeless. May I also be a light in the time of darkness to those who need to hear about You and Your Word. Amen.*

Taking Action

 Plan to help serve a meal to someone in need. Perhaps this could be during the Thanksgiving or Christmas seasons.

 Involve your children and family in taking a meal to a needy family.

Make today a day to have a cheerful spirit for Jesus.

Reading On

Proverbs 15:17   Matthew 10:42
Titus 1:8   Matthew 6:1-4

You can make more friends in two months by becoming interested in other people than you can in two years by trying to get other people interested in you.

—*Dale Carnegie*

Making Time for Stillness

Scripture Reading: Ecclesiastes 3:1-8

Key Verse: Ecclesiastes 3:1

> *There is an appointed time for everything. And there is a time for every event under heaven.*

————— ❦ —————

I know the objection that is already bubbling up in your mind: Who has time?

It's a common complaint—and a valid one.

It's true that the battle is on between Satan and the spirit of stillness. (The father of lies absolutely thrives on chaos and misery!) And it really isn't easy to eliminate all the distractions—the dust, the dirty clothes, the orders that need filing; timers buzzing, phones ringing, children needing us.

But here's what I've discovered: The people who find time for stillness are the people who have the energy and perspective to stay on top of their hectic "outer" lives.

And we're not alone as we struggle to find time for stillness. I truly believe that if we just recognize our daily need, God will help us discover ways to implement our needed quiet times.

Anne Ortlund, whose books on the godly life have influenced a generation of Christian women, tells of a time when she had three children under three and not a spare moment in her day. Longing for a time of quiet with the Lord, she tried desperate measures.

Normally I sleep like a rock, but I said, "Lord, if you'll help me, I'll meet you from two to three a.m." I kept my time with him until the schedule lightened; I didn't die, and I'm not sorry I did it. Everybody has 24 hours. We can soak ourselves in prayer, in his Word, in himself, if we really want to.

With God's help we can do whatever we really want to do and make time for whatever we feel is a priority in our lives. Could you watch TV 25 percent less? Could you get up 15 minutes earlier or half an hour later to take advantage of a quiet house? Could you trade off meal preparation in return for babysitting? With creativity and God's help, you can make space for stillness.

Perhaps the most important means of making time for stillness is the most obvious: Schedule it! Most of us have a tendency to schedule time for work, chores, errands, and family, but leave our quiet time to happenstance. What happens? We manage to take care of work, chores, errands, and family, but somehow the quiet time falls by the wayside!

One friend of mine attended a one-day professional seminar at a cost of 250 dollars. I was eager to find out what was the one most important thing she had learned. She reported that this high-level course had taught her two important things: 1) Make a "to do" list, and 2) on that list, schedule quality time alone each day!

No one else can do it for you; you are the one who must make it and take it for yourself. Purposefully make yourself unavailable to the rest of the world each day and be available to God, yourself, and ultimately to others.

It doesn't have to be a large block of time. Fifteen minutes here and there can save you. Try getting up 15 minutes earlier so you can be utterly alone—or, if you're a night owl, stay up after everyone else is in bed. Ask a neighbor to watch the kids for just half an hour while you lock the bathroom door, sprinkle a few bath crystals in the tub, and enjoy a time of solitude and relaxation. Stake out a table in a quiet coffee shop in between car pool expeditions—or park your car under a quiet tree and enjoy a time of quiet communion with God.

Whenever possible, try to schedule longer quiet time, too. Author and speaker Florence Littauer travels all over the world, yet she will schedule an extra day here and there just to be alone. She orders room service and just enjoys her time reading, thinking, journaling . . . and just spending time with God. I've learned this from Florence and on occasion will do the same thing. I call it my "catch-up" day—time alone to journal, read magazines and newspaper articles, and do other things that refresh my mind and relieve tension. My favorite thing to do for myself is to listen to classical or praise strings, put on a beauty mask, crawl up on our bed, and read *Virtue or Victoria* magazines.

If you have small children, such a "day off for stillness" may seem like an impossible dream. Even 15 minutes of solitude may seem out of reach. And I will admit that those years when little ones have first rights on your time can be a challenge. I know that you can't schedule preschoolers, and help is often hard to find. And yet . . . there really are ways to nuture the spirit of stillness even in the midst of the loveable chaos.[20]

I have to giggle every time I think of what my daughter Jenny used to do to give herself some quiet time. With three children aged two, four, and six, it was pretty difficult to find time for herself. So she put a beauty mask on her face and the faces of all three children. She used a green mud-type mask, since they loved to have green faces with white eyes and rosy lips. Then all three lay face-up on one bed. They knew their mask would crack if they talked or smiled or wiggled, so they lay very still. Jenny then got on the bed with a magazine and put on soft music, and they all relaxed. Often the children would go to sleep. I was amazed that it really worked.

Another day when the children were driving Jenny crazy about 4:30 in the afternoon (the disaster hour), Jenny stripped off their clothes and put all three in a bubble bath. Then she darkened the bathroom, lit a candle, sprayed some cologne, and sat down on the floor to read her Bible. I know it was God who calmed these cute monkeys down and gave Jenny a few moments of stillness. Now the children often ask Mom for a bubble bath with candlelight!

After all, children benefit from the spirit of stillness too. Small ones may seem to generate chaos, but immature nervous systems and bodies weary from the work of growing get the rest they need in an environment of order and peace. We do our children a favor when we teach them to find the spirit of still-ness within themselves and make it a part of their lives.

My Bob and I purposely set aside chunks of our yearly schedule just to be alone with each other and rethink our lives. We work hard all year, fulfilling over a hundred speaking engagements all over the country. Schedules, interviews, and travel keep us on the move. We have to make space for the spirit of stillness, or we would quickly lose track of each other . . . and grow out of touch with God.

The door to stillness really is there waiting for any of us to open it and go through, but it won't open itself. We have to choose to make the spirit of stillness a part of our lives.

I have not always appreciated the value of stillness the way I do now. In fact, I have always been the active, on-the-go type. But I am 50-plus in years now and a grandmother. Finally I am understanding the full importance of quiet time. And it's part of my privilege as a teacher of young women (see Titus 2:4) to share my growing appreciation of the spirit of stillness to show how stillness can enrich our lives and replenish our spirit.

I've come to realize that all people need to get away from everything and everybody on a regular basis for thought, prayer, and just rest. For me this includes both daily quiet times and more extended periods of relaxation and replenishment. And it includes both times spent with my husband and periods of true solitude, spent with just me and God. These times of stillness offer me the chance to look within and nurture the real me. They keep me from becoming frazzled and depleted by the world around me.

I would say the ideal balance between outward and inward pursuit should be about 50-50. By "outward" I mean working toward goals and deadlines, negotiating needs and privileges, coping with stress, taking care of daily chores, striving toward retirement—in other words, getting things done. "Inward" things include tuning in to my spiritual self, talking to God, exploring the sorrows, hopes, and dreams that make up the inner me, and just relaxing in God's eternal presence.

When I was younger, my life was tilted more outward and less inward. As I grow and mature (and perhaps reach another stage of my life), I find I'm leaning more toward the inward. I want my life to be geared more toward heaven. I want to lift my life, my hands, my head, and my body toward God, to spend more time alone with him—talking, listening, and just being. I want to experience the fragrance of His love and let that love permeate my life, to let the calmness of His Spirit replenish the empty well of my heart, which gets depleted in the busyness and rush of the everyday demands and pressures.

I want those things for you, too. That's why I urge you: *Do whatever is necessary to nurture the spirit of stillness in your life.* Don't let the enemy wear you so thin that you lose your balance and perspective. Regular time for stillness is as important and necessary as sleep, exercise, and nutritional food.

Father God, You rested on the seventh day, and I sense a need for more stillness in my life. My nerves and patience wear thin throughout all the demands on my life. When I stop and take time for You, a quietness falls upon me and I can regenerate my battery. I have observed that people do what they want to do, and I want to be STILL. Help me to keep this as a desire of my heart. Amen.

Taking Action

- Dejunk your junkiest room. Clutter wearies the spirit and fights against stillness.

- Keep a Bible, writing paper, and a pen on your bedside table for spiritual food during still moments.

- Make a list of sounds, smells, and places that tend to trigger a spirit of stillness in you.

- Try setting aside a "quiet corner" at home with inspirational books, comfortable cushions, and a warm light.

Reading On

Psalm 37:7	Hebrews 9:28
Isaiah 40:31	Psalm 139:8

Don't pray when you feel like it. Have an appointment with the Lord and keep it. A man is powerful on his knees.

—*Corrie ten Boom*

Make Time for You

Scripture Reading: Matthew 22:34-40

Key Verse: Matthew 22:37,39

> *You shall love the Lord your God with all your heart, and with all your soul, and with all your mind. . . . You shall love your neighbor as yourself.*

God originally gave the above verses of Scripture in Deuteronomy 6:4-9 to the Jewish nation as part of their Shema, which became Judaism's basic confession of faith. According to rabbinic law, this passage was to be recited every morning and night. The passage stresses the uniqueness of God, precludes the worship of other gods, and demands a total love commitment.

In Matthew 22 Jesus was asked, "Teacher, which is the great commandment in the Law?" He gave two commandments which stress three loves: the love of God, the love of self, and the love of your neighbor. In our churches we are taught to love God and to love our neighbors, but we are also taught that we are not to dwell too long on our personal selves. I have found many women who do not know how to care for themselves. As women we always seem to be giving so much to others in our family that there is no time left for us.

As a young woman and a new bride, and then as a new mother, I was always tired. I had no energy left over for me, and we most certainly didn't have enough money left over from our budget to give me anything. So what did I do for myself? Not very much. But after studying this passage of

Scripture, I was challenged to study the subject of personal value in the sight of God—not an overemphasis on self, but a balanced and moderate approach that would let me grow as an individual. I knew that if God was going to make me a complete and functioning person in the body of Christ I had to develop a wholesome approach to this area of caring for myself.

As I began to look about me, I found women who had a mistrust of themselves and had begun to withhold acceptance of themselves—women who had no idea that God had a plan for their lives, so those lives instead reflected fear, guilt, and mistrust of other people.

In the 1990's, awareness of the whole topic of the dysfunctional family let us realize that many of us come from a family with some sort of abnormality. We begin to manifest those early childhood fears, guilt, and mistrust of others because we don't want to be hurt, scared, or disappointed again. Along with these manifestations, Satan makes us believe that we are totally worthless as persons, and certainly not worthy to spend any extra time or money on.

As I looked around in my association with women at church, support groups, and home Bible studies, I found many women who did not understand that God had given them a certain divine dignity at birth. The women would relate to their friends either positively or negatively depending on how well they understood this principle.

One Friday morning while we were studying a marriage book, Amy spoke up and said that she didn't take care of her personal self because her father had told her when she was young that pretty girls with good clothes and a nice figure stood a better chance of being molested by older boys and men as they grew up.

At that time Amy decided she would not let herself be molested by an older man, so she began to gain weight, wear sloppy clothes, and certainly not look good in a bathing suit. She even remarked that her husband liked her this way because then other men didn't try to flirt with her. He was safe from any competition, and he liked that.

Over the next several months in our weekly study I began to share how this fear was put there by Satan and not by God. I took extra time encouraging her to be all that God had for her. We looked at her eating habits and why she chose certain foods. (She also sought special counseling to understand what she was hiding behind.) Today Amy is a fine young lady who has a totally new image and who shares with other women her confidence in caring for herself. Because of Amy's self-appraisal, her husband has also joined a support group at church and has lessened his fears from his own insecurities.

Paul teaches in Philippians 4:13, "I can do all things through Him who strengthens me." In using this principle we realize that Christ gives us the inner strength to care for ourselves. Time for ourselves gives us time to reflect on the renewal of our mind, body, and spirit. Not only will we be rewarded personally, but so will all who come in contact with us daily.

> *Father God, I am special because of You and Your grace. You have taught me who I am, and out of my thanksgiving to You daily, You have given me a thankful heart. Through this I realize who I am in Your eyes: a person created in Your likeness. You have showed me how to take time for myself, and it is so meaningful. I know I enjoy life more than I used to. Amen.*

Taking Action

❧ Next time you take a walk, pick a few flowers. Tuck them in a vase by your bed.

❧ Dust the sheets with baby powder or sweet perfume before crawling into bed. You'll enjoy a welcome sense of relaxation as well as a feeling that is absolutely beautiful.

❦ Hang a tuneful wind chime out on the patio and enjoy its music on breezy days.

❦ Enjoy a bubble bath by candlelight while sipping ice tea or a pleasing beverage.

Reading On

Psalm 40:1-3   Deuteronomy 6:4-9
Psalm 42:1,2   Matthew 19:19

If you want to be respected by others, the great thing is to respect yourself.

—*Fyodor Dostoevsky*

Your Days Are Written in God's Book

Scripture Reading: Psalm 139:16-18

Key Verse: Psalm 139:16

> *Thine eyes have seen my unformed substance [embryo];*
> *and in Thy book they were all written, the days that were*
> *ordained for me, when as yet there was not one of them.*

It was the day our daughter was leaving for college, and we both looked forward to it with anticipation. Excitement wasn't quite the word for how we both felt, because Jenny was leaving home to a new adventure, while for me it meant an empty nest with a quiet household.

Her blue Volkswagen bug was all packed now, so down the hill she drove, tooting her horn as she went into the sunset. I walked slowly up the porch steps into the house. It was quiet at last—no loud stereo, no popcorn on the floor, no pizza on the counter, no teenagers around the house, no telephones ringing. My parenting years were over, now that both our children were in college. I made a quick swing through the house to put it in order, only to discover that it was already in order. My organizational skills had been in full swing, and somehow the children had learned them also. My Bob was building a mobile home manufacturing company at the time, which was consuming much of his time. It didn't seem like he needed me.

All at once I realized I wasn't needed anymore. My children didn't need me, my Bob didn't need me, and my house didn't need me. So now what? All that I loved was now ending.. I loved my mothering, my organizing, my cleaning, and my cooking. But now it was just me and a part-time Bob.

Little did I know that God's plan was already in progress, as our Scripture for today states. My days were ordained to me before they even began. My homemaking and domestic engineering days were all a part of the training that God had poured into my life, for this was to be our future ministry to families.

I'm grateful that I was an at-home mom, for now with an empty nest I had time to move ahead with the rest of God's plan for me. Because of my friend and mentor Florence Littauer, I was encouraged to write my first book. Then came more books. In 1982 Bob closed his mobile home company to work with me and build God's ministry of "More Hours in My Day."

Whatever the degree of involvement and however the relationship works itself out, the command is clear: Older women [are] to live for God's glory.

—*Susan Hunt*

I say all this to encourage you today. Whatever you may be experiencing at the present time is all a part of what God has for you in the future, as long as you are willing to allow Him to teach your heart and guide your steps. I would never have thought that a shy and fearful little Jewish girl with just a high school education could write over 22 books and speak on platforms in conferences all over the country. In my own power I still can't do it, but in the power of the Lord we can all do the impossible.

Father God, encourage that woman today who has read this devotion. Give her Your love, strength, and power. And give her the allotted days to develop, learn,

and achieve what You would have her to do and become.
You have certainly given me far more than I ever expected. Amen.

Taking Action

❦ Write in your journal your goals for the next six
  months of your personal future.

❦ Thank God today for what He is teaching you. You
  will need these things for the future.

❦ Submit yourself to God today, and ask Him to create
  in you the woman He wants you to be.

Reading On

Romans 8:29   Acts 2:23
Romans 11:2   1 Peter 1:20

Man's highest reward for his
dedication to the pursuit of excellence is not what he gets
from it, but what he becomes
through it.

—*Author Unknown*

□ □ □

Who, Me Change?

Scripture Reading: John 8:28-36

Key Verse: John 8:32

You shall know the truth, and the truth shall make you free.

One foggy night the captain of a large ship saw what appeared to be another ship's lights approaching in the distance. This other ship was on a course that would mean a head-on crash. Quickly the captain signaled to the approaching ship, "Please change your course 10 degrees west." The reply came blinking back through the thick fog, "You change your course 10 degrees east."

Indignantly the captain pulled rank and shot a message back to the other ship, "I'm a sea captain with 35 years of experience. You change your course 10 degrees west!" Without hesitation the signal flashed back, "I'm a seaman fourth-class. You change your course 10 degrees east!"

Enraged and incensed, the captain realized that within minutes they would crash head-on, so he blazed his final warning back to the fast-approaching ship: "I'm a 50,000-ton freighter. You change your course 10 degrees west!" The simple message winked back, "I'm a lighthouse. You change. . . ."[21]

As a young bride of 17, I wasn't aware of the differences between a man and a woman even though I had been raised in a home with an older brother. I just figured that my Bob would think just like I did. After all, wasn't I raised with everything being right? If there were differences, it must be because Bob did things strangely. Just to show what contrasts we brought to the marriage, I will list a few.

Emilie

1. Raised Jewish
2. Did whatever we wanted on Sundays
3. Ate leg of lamb, rice, rye bread, cream cheese
4. Father passed away when I was eleven
5. Father was alcoholic
6. Lived in an apartment all my life
7. Commuted on a public bus
8. Older brother was in trouble
9. Enjoyed sleeping in until 10 or 11 o'clock on Saturday mornings

Bob

1. Raised Baptist
2. Went to church on Sundays and observed Christian holidays
3. Ate fried chicken, mashed potatoes, gravy and biscuits
4. Had an encouraging and supportive father
5. Father abstained from alcohol
6. Lived in a residential home
7. Had a family car
8. Two brothers were achievers
9. Was an early riser regardless of day of week

These are just a few of our differences. Needless to say, we needed to make some compromises and adjustments! If either of us had demanded that our marriage reflect only our own values, we would certainly have crashed into the lighthouse and our ship would have been smashed on the rocks of the shore.

Even before we were married, we had to settle our differences regarding our spiritual beliefs. Bob had asked my mother if I could go to church with him, and surprisingly she said yes. That started me on my search for truth.

After many months of reading, listening, and praying I had a real peace that Jesus was who He said He was. Our key verse for today stood out so clearly that the truth did set me free. Verse 36 states, "If therefore the Son shall make you free, you shall be free indeed." From that very moment, at 16 years of age, I responded to the Master's call, corrected my course in life, and was amazingly free for every other change in life.

You too may be at a fork in the road of your life. Because of past experiences, you and your husband may not want to budge from your respective positions. I petition both of you today to come to grips with what is holding you a prisoner and to be set free by Christ's atonement for your sins on the cross.

Once you have come to grips with this issue, all other changes seem minor. With some things in life it makes no difference how you do them, but this spiritual change is a pivotal point around which all other changes take place.

Satan would like to destroy our marriage relationships because of differences in the way we like to do things. But we must be willing to serve one another. One of our guiding principles when it comes to change is found in Ephesians 5:21: "Be subject to one another." We each want to serve rather than be served. Each day our prayer is "How can we serve each other today?" With that daily attitude we are free to serve each other in a mature, godly fashion. Anything less than this allows selfishness and pride to enter our lives and ultimately creates an unwillingness to make changes.

Yes, I now like fried chicken and Bob loves a good leg of lamb. Be willing to change your course rather than have your own way by ramming into the lighthouse!

Father God, thank You for a heart that is willing to be flexible and to make changes in life. I don't want to always be right; I want to be free. I cry when I see couples who are so rigid in their ways, for I know what the end will be for them and their family. The consequences of stubbornness will be felt for many generations. I pray for a pliable heart. Continue to give me a serving heart. Amen.

Taking Action

- In your journal, make a chart listing your differences with your mate.

- Beside each difference state briefly how it is being resolved.

- For each one not resolved, set a time to meet with your mate to see if there are any changes to be made.

- Resolve those differences that can be, and continue to pray for those that aren't.

Reading On

Genesis 24:48   John 16:13
Psalm 91:4   2 Timothy 2:25

When I came to believe in Christ's teachings, I ceased desiring what I had wished for before. The direction of my life, my desires, became different. What was good and bad changed places.

—*Leo Tolstoy*

If Talking the Talk, Walk the Walk

Scripture Reading: Matthew 7:1-5

Key Verse: Matthew 7:3

Why do you look at the speck that is in your brother's eye, but do not notice the log that is in your own eye?

———— ❧ ————

Hypocrisy is a dangerous character trait. Hypocrites are those who say one thing and do another. This is so dangerous because after a while of acting this way they become immune to the whole enterprise. It becomes, for them, just a natural way to live.

However, they do not allow others to live that way. This type of person is the first one to protest when they themselves are hurt by the actions of others who hypocritically approach life. This does not make much sense, does it?

Many years ago, grocers bought their supplies from the local townspeople. They then sold them to those who shopped in their stores. The suppliers, meanwhile, bartered for the things that they needed exchanged for the supplies.

Once there was a woman named Mary who bartered butter with one of the local grocers. Mary had the best butter in the area. She dealt almost all of the time with George down at the market. He bought her butter and traded with her for other things that she needed.

Their arrangement was based on Mary weighing out the butter and bringing it to George. Each pound of butter was worth so much in money or other things from George's store. It was a mutually satisfying arrangement that lasted for quite some time.

After a number of months of dealing with each other, George called the town sheriff and made a complaint. He charged Mary with cheating him in the weight of her butter. The grocer seemed to be sincerely shocked that Mary would do such a thing. The sheriff called Mary to George's store, where George confronted her with his charge.

"For the past four weeks Mary has cheated me two ounces in every pound of butter that she traded with me. I waited this long to say anything to see if she had simply made a mistake once or twice. But now I see that each pound of butter that she brings me is short these two ounces. I cannot believe that someone, especially Mary, would do such a thing!"

Mary responded, "That sure is curious. Four weeks ago I lost my pound weight that I used to weigh the butter. I started using the pound of soap that I bought from you as the weight measure for the butter." George said no more about the butter. He was caught red-handed.

There is an old statement that fits well here: "Clean your own backyard before you try to clean someone else's."[22]

Life without a standard has a tendency to be tossed and turned. It becomes confused because it has faith in an object that can't be relied upon. When Mary lost her benchmark, the pound weight, instead of purchasing an absolute pound weight she substituted George's soap weight. She thought this was a true measurement, not realizing that George had underweighed his soap in order to cheat those who traded with him.

In this story and with today's Scripture reading, I find two lessons to be learned.

First, our actions need to be consistent with our talk. If we are going to take a stand on moral issues, we must be sure that our stand is consistent with our life. I often wonder if all the various activists in life really walk their talk. Jesus used the term "hypocrite" when He described the insincerity of the Pharisees and scribes.

When we are bold and take a basic position on the moral issues of life, we need to have a clean slate regarding our own character record. Our country is currently debating the issue of a person's character. Is it important for a person to have good character in order to be a leader of people? Many people in this country are willing to let character slide as long as the person is able to make good choices outside the moral arena.

The Scriptures are quite clear on the issue of consistency in our lives. As parents we realize that our young ones are watching Mommy and Daddy to make sure we walk our talk. If we don't, the children will recognize that we are frauds, and will want no part of our hypocrisy.

The second lesson I see is taken from the story of George and Mary. Mary lost her object of faith, the pound weight, and substituted another standard of measurement, the soap bar. Without investigating or checking out the new standard, she put her faith in this new object. Even though she was totally sincere in relying on this new standard, she was 100 percent wrong in her blind faith.

Today in our Western culture there are many claims that seem to be right: They "feel good," the people seem sincere, they are well-dressed, etc. But their object of faith is wrong. They have lost sight of Jesus and His Word and have been led astray by thinking they are okay.

If we stray away from the real Jesus, we become a victim of hypocrisy. We need to keep our eyes on Jesus and accept no substitute.

Mother, if you are going to talk the talk, make sure you walk the walk. Don't worry about the speck in other people's eyes, but be willing to remove the log out of your own eye first. If you don't, others around you will point out the log for you.

> *Father God, as You bring before me today the importance of having a pure heart before You and my family, I want You to remove the log out of my own eye. Bring before me those parts of my life that aren't consistent with your Word. I really want to be a good and faithful servant. I want to stand before You with a life that is consistent with my talk. I don't want just hot air coming from my lips. Amen.*

Taking Action

 Look in a mirror and study yourself. What do you see? Write in your journal what you see.

 Look beyond your face and into your heart. Now what do you see? Jot those thoughts down too.

 Is what you see consistent with what you say you are? If not, where are the differences?

 What are you going to do to narrow this conflict?

Reading On

Job 20:4,5	Romans 12:9
Luke 12:1	1 Peter 2:1

No man, for any considerable period, can wear one face to himself and another to the multitude, without finally getting bewildered as to which may be true.

—*Nathaniel Hawthorne*

❑ ❑ ❑

How to Raise Delinquent Children

Scripture Reading: Proverbs 22:1-6

Key Verse: Proverbs 22:6
Train up a child in the way he should go, [and] even when he is old he will not depart from it.

"Strict parent" is not a very good phrase to use at social gatherings today. From my observations of some children raised in the church, it isn't even politically correct within the confines of *that* institution! One can easily observe in a child's behavior if his or her parents have limitations within the confines of their home.

One of the easiest tip-offs on this topic is to see with what respect the child speaks to his or her parents. Many children today show little respect when addressing the adults in their lives, whether teacher, coach, policeman, pastor, or parent. When we see such behavior, we know that these children come from a home that is not strict.

In all types of situations we read or hear about the sad results when a child is allowed to roam without any boundaries. One of the saddest results is when we hear of a child losing his or her life because he was never required to heed the warning of a parent.

A family had taken shelter in the basement as a severe storm passed over their town. The radio warned that a tornado had been spotted. When the storm had passed by, the father opened the front door to look at the damage. A downed power line was whipping dangerously on the street in front of their house. Before the father realized what was happening, his five-year-old daughter ran right by him, headed for that sparkling wire in the street.

"Laurie, stop!" he yelled.

Laurie just kept going.

"Laurie, STOP!"

Laurie ran right for the enticing cable.

"STOP NOW, Laurie!"

Little Laurie reached down to pick up the wicked power line and was instantly killed.

What a heartbreaking tragedy! But the real tragedy is that this happened because a little girl had never been taught that when her father said no, he really meant no. It cost him the life of his daughter.[23]

What a tragedy when a senseless death occurs because a child has never learned to obey! No is such a simple word, but so difficult to obey.

The world has painted the word "strict" as child abuse, as robbing a child of his free spirit so he won't become himself. But in reality, "strict" is a word that develops focus, discipline, achievement, peace, balance, and success in life.

As our children, Brad and Jennifer, have become older, they thank us for giving them boundaries when they were in their formative years. They knew that Mom and Dad loved them, were affectionate to them, verbally praised them, and emotionally supported them. In fact, in many areas of child-rearing our children are stricter with their own children than we were with them.

Several years ago the Houston, Texas, Police Department sponsored a large public-relations campaign to combat the rising tide in juvenile crime. Chuck Swindoll in his book *You and Your Child* relates one of the most effective messages in this campaign, "Twelve Rules for Raising Delinquent Children":

1. Begin with infancy to give the child everything he wants. In this way he will grow up to believe the world owes him a living.

2. When he picks up bad words, laugh at him. This will make him think he's cute.

3. Never give him any spiritual training. Wait until he is 21 and then let him "decide for himself."

4. Avoid the use of "wrong." He may develop a guilt complex. This will condition him to believe later, when he is arrested for stealing a car, that society is against him and he is being persecuted.

5. Pick up everything he leaves lying around. Do everything for him so that he will be experienced in throwing all responsibility on others.

6. Let him read any printed matter he can get his hands on. Be careful that the silverware and drinking glasses are sterilized, but let his mind feast on garbage.

7. Quarrel frequently in the presence of your children. In this way they won't be so shocked when the home is broken up later.

8. Give a child all the spending money he wants. Never let him earn his own.

9. Satisfy his every craving for food, drink, and comfort. See that his every sensual desire is gratified.

10. Take his part against neighbors, teachers, and policemen. They are all prejudiced against your child.

11. When he gets into real trouble, apologize for yourself by saying, "I could never do anything with him."

12. Prepare for a life of grief. You will be likely to have it.[24]

You and your spouse need to decide today what effects you want to have on your children. Also remember that how they live today is more than likely how their next three generations will live. It is up to us as parents to stand in the gap and hang tough. This is not an easy battle, for the evil one would like you to give in to the path of least resistance, but you must be willing to travel the "road less traveled."

> *Father God, thanks for encouraging me today that being strict is okay and that the pressure I receive from others means I'm doing a good job in establishing the boundaries in our home. I wish there were an easier way to raise well-behaved children, but I see that there aren't any. I appreciate my caring attitude so that I'm motivated to endure all the backlash. I ask that You put into the hearts of my children a sense of obedience to authority. I so very much want them to care. Please put a protective hedge around their little lives. Amen.*

Taking Action

- ❧ Each day for the next two weeks meet with your spouse and review one of the 12 rules to see how you're doing in each area.

- ❧ After studying number 12, rank in order the three rules that need the most work in your household.

- ❧ After each of the three rules, jot down what you are going to do that will turn the negative into a positive.

Reading On

Hebrews 12:9-11	Ephesians 6:4
Proverbs 29:1	Proverbs 22:15

———————— ❧ ————————

My father was a Methodist and believed in the laying on of hands, and believe me, he really laid them on!

—A.W. Tozer

———————— ❧ ————————

□ □ □

Being an Older Woman Is Exciting

Scripture Reading: Titus 2:3-10

Key Verse: Titus 2:4

Encourage the young women to love their husbands, to love their children.

———— ❦ ————

As a young woman and mother, I would read today's Scripture passage and totally disregard the part about the older women teaching the younger women. I just never thought I would be older! However, 35-plus years later, I'm very pleased today to be the older woman teaching younger women. In fact, we are all older to someone. Even our 13-year-old granddaughter teaches the ones she babysits.

I am the person I am today because of the many godly women in my life. I have been taught by older women who didn't even know they were teaching me. I would (and still do) watch others in the ways they dealt with problems, organized their homes, and entertained, and especially in the way they walked with God. I hope I never get to the point where I stop learning.

I remember one older woman who sat in the front row of the church when I was teaching a "More Hours in My Day" seminar. She took notes the whole time. I later found out she was 92 years old! I thought, "At 92, who cares about organization?" But she truly had a teachable spirit, and I'm sure she went out to teach them to someone else. I later found out that she also had had a goal in her life to water ski, so at 90 years of age she did so and lived to tell about it!

Passing on ways to love our husbands is so exciting. I have learned from many women in my life some creative ways to show love to my Bob: a note of appreciation in a lunchbag or on the computer; a phone call just to say "I care," "I'm praying," "I'm making your favorite dessert," or just "I love you"; a thank you for working so long and hard for our family, for being a great dad, for stepping in the gap when I'm at work to make dinner or water the flowerpots or vacuum.

I've learned that a man needs to be admired and appreciated even for the small things. Even if your husband doesn't do any of the above, find something (and you can) that you admire him for. The more he knows you appreciate him, the more he'll do for you. The old saying still holds true, "Treat him as a king and he'll treat you as a queen." Side by side you can complete each other and not compete with each other.

As an older woman, I'm thankful for a mother who taught me meal-planning, shopping, cooking, cleaning, sewing, hospitality, and much more. Today I'm passing this on to the seminar women and those who read my books, as well as to my children and my children's children.

Yes, being an older woman is rewarding. The younger women are excited and eager to learn from us. What a joyful privilege God has given us!

Training younger women in the church is an important part of the responsibility of spiritually mature women. The mentoring relationship should not be formal, rigid, or overly structured, but should be a warm, indirect, motherly approach. Our main goal is to show these younger women how to live out the gospel in a lifestyle that is pleasing and truthful to God's Word.

Our balanced lifestyle that endures the test of time is what is caught by the young women around us. Even though we may not feel skilled in this area, we need to be risk-takers in sharing what God has entrusted to us.

Father God, thank You for older women who are willing to teach what You have taught them through life's experiences. May we always be open to the hearts of those who have teachable spirits. Help those of us who have husbands to show them how much we love and appreciate them. Most of all, Lord, help us to become friends with Your Word, the Bible, and to step out and teach what we have learned. Amen.

Taking Action

- ❦ List in your journal the women you know whom you can mentor.

- ❦ List in your journal three things you appreciate about your husband, father, son, or brother.

- ❦ List 10 things you can teach your children which someday they can pass on to someone else.

Reading On

Ruth 2:20-22   Luke 1:56
Luke 1:41-45   Acts 18:24-28

Having sought for so long the real meaning and key to life, and having found it in Jesus, I couldn't keep quiet about this discovery. Everybody had to know!

—*Geoffrey Shaw*

The Spirit of Creativity

Scripture Reading: 2 Corinthians 5:14-21

Key Verse: 2 Corinthians 5:17

If any man is in Christ, he is a new creature; the old things passed away; behold, new things have come.

———— ❦ ————

I've heard it a million times, expressed with admiration and usually a little envy: "Oh, she's so creative."

Usually it describes an "artsy" type of person—someone who paints or writes or makes pottery. Such creative pursuits can bring great joy to those who do them and to those who enjoy the results. But you really don't have to be an artist to infuse your home and life with the spirit of creativity.

Creativity is a God-given ability to take something ordinary and make it into something special. It is an openness to doing old things in new ways and a willingness to adapt other people's good ideas to suit our personal needs. And creativity is an ability we all possess, although many of us keep it hidden in the deep corners of our lives.

Every human being is creative. The creative spirit is part of our heritage as children of the One who created all things. And nurturing our creativity is part of our responsibility as stewards of God's good gifts.

Creativity is so much more than just "arts and crafts." It is a way of seeing, a willingness to see wonderful possibilities in something unformed or ordinary or even ugly.

The first year Bob and I moved to Riverside, California, where we now live, we went to our first auction in an old building near Mount Rubidoux. It was fun to see the various "treasures" that were up for sale—everything from armoires to yarn caddies—and to listen as the auctioneer shouted the calls. Then an old, greasy market scale went up, and Bob shouted a bid. I nearly died on the spot. Whatever did he think we would do with that?

He won the bid and paid 32 dollars for that ugly old scale. We went to pick it up, and I looked at it doubtfully, but Bob was sure he had bought a treasure. And he was right! He stripped the old scale clean, shined and polished it until it looked almost new, and then put it on a table. That was over 20 years ago, and we are still enjoying Bob's imaginative purchase. It graces the narrow table behind our sofa and carries fruit in its tray, or sometimes a pot of flowers, a bowl of potpourri, or a Boston fern. Over the years, as we continue to shop for antiques, we often see scales not nearly as nice as ours that cost hundreds of dollars. I'm so grateful to Bob for his creative input into our home.

One day Bob brought me another treasure from one of his antique sprees. It was a large, wooden, hand-carved rectangular bowl—another of those "What will I ever do with that thing?" items. But how I enjoy that bowl as it sits on our butcher block island in the center of our kitchen! I keep it full of potatoes, onions, avocados, oranges, lemons, apples, and a variety of other fruits. It's not only beautiful, but very practical—another example of Bob's "creative seeing."

The kind of vision that brings the special out of the ordinary has long been part of the American tradition. Even in the tiniest frontier cabin, pioneer women found ways to express their creative urges and to add touches of loveliness to their environment.

In great-grandma's day, quilting was a wonderfully creative pursuit for women in many areas of the country. When women married or had a baby, friends and families gathered together to make the quilts the new family needed to keep warm. They used old, discarded clothing which was cut up and patched together into colorful designs and then carefully padded and stitched to make warm coverings. The women worked, talked, and exchanged recipes; they solved garden, food, husband, and children problems—all while their hard-working fingers sewed. These quilts were truly labors of love—living testaments to the spirit of loveliness that transforms simple materials and a basic household need into a work of art and an occasion for celebration.

Our human ability to create differs from that of God's in that

- He created the world out of nothing;
- His creativity is unlimited (Genesis 1:1-2:3).

We are limited to doing what is in our existing natural world. Our creativity has to be expressed by thought and experience. Our manifestations are shown in our creative forms of music, art, literature, language, or problem-solving; in creating a new idea, adapting a recipe, or stretching a monthly budget. There are many ways for us humans to express ourselves with our creativity.

We tend to think we need to be original in order to be creative. But I'm continually getting ideas from magazines, decorator shops, programs on the Discovery channel, interviewing friends, and just keeping my eyes open to life. I must be willing to make changes in the way things have always been done. I can't be satisfied with status quo.

I have found that creative people are focused, committed, and disciplined in their lives. In short, they have a plan for their lives. They know where they want to go, and most of them take control of their lives and live it out God's way.

Each of us is to look inward to see what gifts God has given us. The Scriptures teach us to realize that we have divinely appointed abilities.

Don't be afraid of failure because failure is often a stepping-stone to future successes. Failure can give us new direction in solving a particular problem.

Our home can be a wonderful laboratory in which to express our God-given talent. We can open this window in many ways:

- Landscaping
- Cooking
- Decorating
- Home business
- Parenting
- Marriage
- Designing and sewing clothes
- Arts and crafts
- Painting
- Composing
- Writing

One of the most valuable ways we can share the spirit of creativity is by modeling it for our children. We give them a legacy of joy when we teach them to use their God-given creativity to instill the spirit of loveliness into their own lives and homes.

Exercising our creativity is one way for us to be responsible stewards of the gifts and talents God has given us, and to rejoice in our identity as God's children, made in His image. As images of the Creator, we have the opportunity to fashion our lives and our homes into works of art. We can choose to be creative today and every day!

> *Father God, thank You for giving me my talents and for letting me have a spirit of loveliness. I can't paint, sing, draw, sculpture, design, or play an instrument, but I can dare to experiment with other talents. As such, people look at me and think I'm creative. So if my friends mirror back to me that I'm creative, I must be. Thanks for giving me friends who help me put my best foot forward. My desire is to encourage other women to step out and dare to be creative.*

Nothing is more exciting to see than someone trying to fly when You have encouraged her to extend her wings and flap. Amen.

Taking Action

❦ Use your imagination in displaying your collection of cups and saucers, bells, dolls, thimbles, or salt-and-pepper shakers. A side table, shelf, or armoire can serve beautifully, but so might a printer's tray, a special basket, or a windowsill. One friend of mine displayed her collection of teddy bears in a clean but nonfunctioning fireplace.

❦ If you don't have a collection, start one! You'll have fun, and your family and friends will never lack for gift-giving ideas. Some more ideas: pitchers, cookie jars, music boxes. One academically minded gentleman collects university T-shirts. (He displays his collection on himself!)

❦ Throw a pretty tablecloth over your coffee table and serve hors d'oeuvres, tea, coffee, or dessert in the living room or den instead of the dining room or kitchen. Or try setting up a card table for dinner in the garden. Your family or your guests will love the change of pace.

Reading On

1 Peter 4:19	Romans 12:6-8
Romans 1:25	Proverbs 24

Since there is nothing new under the sun, creativity means simply putting old things together in a fresh way.

—*Author Unknown*

She Became My Mirror

Scripture Reading: Ephesians 3:13-21

Key Verse: Ephesians 3:20

To Him who is able to do exceeding abundantly beyond all that we ask or think, according to the power that works within us.

Peter Foster was a Royal Air Force pilot. These men (pilots) were the cream of the crop of England—the brightest, healthiest, most confident and dedicated, and often the most handsome men in the country. When they walked the streets in their decorated uniforms, the population treated them as gods. All eyes turned their way. Girls envied those who were fortunate enough to walk beside a man in Air Force blue.

However, the scene in London was far from romantic, for the Germans were attacking relentlessly. Fifty-seven consecutive nights they bombed London. In waves of 250, some 1500 bombers would come each evening and pound the city.

The RAF Hurricanes and Spitfires that pilots like Foster flew looked like mosquitoes pestering the huge German bombers. The Hurricane was agile and effective, yet it had one fatal design flaw: The single-propeller engine was mounted in front, a scant foot or so from the cockpit, and the fuel lines snaked alongside the cockpit toward the engine. In a direct hit, the cockpit would erupt into an inferno of flames. The pilot could eject, but in the one or two seconds it took him to find the lever, heat would melt off every feature of his face: his nose, his eyelids, his lips, often his cheeks.

These RAF heroes many times would undergo a series of 20 to 40 surgeries to refashion what was once their face. Plastic surgeons worked miracles, yet what remained of the face was essentially a scar.

Peter Foster became one of these "downed pilots." After numerous surgical procedures, what remained of his face was indescribable. The mirror he peered into daily couldn't hide the facts. As the day for his release from the hospital grew closer, so did Peter's anxiety about being accepted by his family and friends.

He knew that one group of airmen with similar injuries had returned home only to be rejected by their wives and girlfriends. Some of the men were divorced by wives who were unable to accept this new outer image of their husbands. Some men became recluses, refusing to leave their houses.

In contrast, there was another group who returned home to families who gave loving assurance of acceptance and continued worth. Many became executives and professionals, leaders in their communities.

Peter Foster was in that second group. His girlfriend assured him that nothing had changed except a few millimeters' thickness of skin. She loved him, not his facial membrane, she assured him. The two were married just before Peter left the hospital.

"She became my mirror," Peter said of his wife. "She gave me a new image of myself. Even now, regardless of how I feel, when I look at her she gives me a warm, loving smile that tells me I am O.K." he tells confidently.[25]

We as women reflect to our mates and children acceptance or rejection by our verbal and nonverbal communications. They pick up from us what they are in life. In order for our family to feel worthy within themselves they need people around them that reflect acceptance.

It takes so little to make us glad,
Just a cheering clasp of a friendly
hand, Just a word from one who
can understand; And we finish
the task we long had planned,
And we lose the doubt and the
fear we had—So little it takes to
make us glad.

—*Ida Goldsmith Morris*

Negative reflection builds fear in one's self. We see a nation built on fear. As we observe teenagers at school or at our local mall, we see many of them who radiate the dullness of fear. Your husband, too, will not be able to make good leadership decisions if he lacks confidence in his decision-making ability. But if you give him encouraging words that build him up, then you as his mirror tell him he's okay. (See Ephesians 4:29.)

Our families will exhibit changed personalities when they are no longer captured by the fear of rejection. In 1 John 4:18 we read that "perfect love casts out fear."

People will reflect back to you with what they live:

- People who live with praise reflect confidence.

- People who live with challenges and responsibilities grow up making proper goals and decisions.

- People who live with optimism aren't afraid to try.

- People who live with love learn to give their love away.

- People are glad to be alive when they realize they are a valuable member of a team.

As your husband and children look at you, may they be freed from fear because they are assured they have a valuable place in the family structure. Reassure them each day through your words and deeds that you love them more than anything else.

Recently our daughter, Jenny, sent this birthday card to my Bob. In part it said:

> All my life you've always been there,
> Helping, advising, and showing you care,
> And all my life I'll always be glad
> To have someone as special as you for my Dad!
> Thank you for the unconditional love you show me.
> I love you—#1 daughter,
>
> Jenny

Here was a father who was blessed for having mirrored back to his daughter that she was accepted, even though many times there was pain in Bob's life because of some of her decisions.

I challenge you today to clean off the smudges and fingerprints on your mirror and to start a fresh image with sharp, clean reflections on your mirror of life. Be a builder, not a destroyer.

> *Father God, I want to be the kind of woman that reflects Your love in all that I do. Sometimes my eyes see what I don't like to see, the action breaks my heart, and I fall asleep with tears in my eyes. I know You are in control and I will prayfully trust You in all things. I want to believe in the goodness even when I can't physically see it. May my family see You reflected back when they see my life lived out before them. Amen.*

Taking Action

- Take each member of your family aside this week and tell them how much they mean to you.

- Make a favorite dessert for family appreciation night.

- In your journal, write down three things that you are going to do in the next three months to mirror your acceptance of each of your family members in your life.

Reading On

Ephesians 4:29   James 3:7,8

The best things are nearest:
breath in the nostrils, light in
your eyes, flowers at your feet,
duties at your hand, the part of
God just before you.

—*Robert Louis Stevenson*

God Is in Control

Scripture Reading: Philippians 1:1-6

Key Verse: Philippians 1:6

I am confident of this very thing, that He who began a good work in you will perfect it until the day of Christ Jesus.

At a recent seminar we attended, the speaker was giving illustrations on control within a family. Some participants thought various members and acts of the family showed who had control. Comments included:

- The breadwinner of the family has control.
- Mom does because she makes more money.
- The one who signs the checks has control.
- The one who pays the bill at the restaurant when we go out to eat has control.
- The husband has control because he is responsible for the family.

After several more comments were written on the board, a strong male voice in the middle of the audience shouted out, "The one who controls the TV clicker has control!" Everyone laughed, knowing that he was on the right path in most families. Who would ever have thought this statement might really have some validity in our homes? If it is really true, then we have lost sight of God's intent on family leadership.

In today's study Paul is teaching believers some basic principles on partnership in ministry. He wants us to see the power of God and how He truly is the One in control. Yet so many homes are wracked with a power struggle in deciding who is in control at 1001 West Maple Street.

If we can grasp today's lesson from God's perspective, we can get a better handle on this awesome question, "Who is in control?" If our family is truly a partnership, we will be enacting several components of that partnership taken from today's reading:

- Thank God for all your remembrance of each family member (verse 3).

- Offer prayers with joy (verse 4).

- Each member is an active participant in the gospel (verse 5).

- There is a perspective of confidence for the future (verse 6).

- He who began a good work in you will perfect it until Jesus returns (verse 6).

Such teamwork leads to confidence in the future. The glue that makes all this happen is the One who will perfect your good work when Jesus returns—the Almighty God. It's so refreshing to know that the possessor of the TV clicker is not ultimately in control. (If it *were* true, I couldn't have much confidence in what God is capable of doing in my life!)

God is the potter and I am the clay, and He can do with me whatever He wishes in my life. In all of life's ups and downs, I don't really need the answer to the question "Why, God? Why me?" Instead, I will be more inclined to say, "Why *not* me, God?"

Yes, God is in control and He has done a wonderful job over the centuries. If we are part of His team, we know that we are in good hands. He knows the beginning from the end, and He is more capable of making the right decision than we are.

> *Father God, over the years I have learned to trust You more. Each time I'm tempted to take control of the events of my life I have to reflect back over all the things You have decided for me, and they were good. May I always be willing to be the clay and for You to design me in Your own way. I gladly give my life to You. Thank You for being so dependable. Amen.*

Taking Action

- List in your journal five things in your life that you have given over to God.
- List three things that you are still controlling.
- Today give those three things to God and do not grab them back.
- Share your decision with a friend and ask her to hold you accountable for it.

Reading On

Proverbs 16:4   1 Corinthians 1:8
Romans 9:21   Romans 8:28

We cooperate with God through obedience, believing that the moment we step out in that obedience the Holy Spirit will meet us with the necessary power.

—*Sandy Smith*

☐ ☐ ☐

A Moment of Grace

Scripture Reading: Ephesians 2:1-9

Key Verse: Ephesians 2:8,9

By grace you have been saved, through faith; and that not of yourselves, it is the gift of God; not as a result of works, that no one should boast.

In the following story we can see the power of grace at work . . .

During my senior year in high school I had been sick with bronchitis and missed two weeks of school. When I returned I had to make up nine tests in one week. By the last one I was really out of it. I remember looking at this test paper and not knowing any of the answers. I was a total blank. It was like I had never heard of this history junk before.

It was after school and I was the only one in the classroom. The teacher was working at his desk and I was staring off into space. "What's the matter?" he asked. And I said, "I can't do this. I don't know any of these answers." He got up and came over and looked at my paper and said, "You know the answer to that! We just talked about it in class yesterday. You answered a question I asked about that." I said, "I don't remember. I just can't remember." He gave me a few hints, but I still couldn't remember. I realized that I was on overload, and my straight A's in history were now a thing of the past. I looked at him and I said,

"Look. You're just gonna have to give me an F. I can't do it. I feel too bad." He reached down with his red pencil and I watched him, certain he was going to put an F on my paper—I mean, there was not one answer on this test! But he put an A on the top.

I said, "What are you doing?" And he said, "If you'd been here and you felt good and you'd had time to study, that's what you'd have gotten. So that's what you're gonna get." This guy really did recognize that I had been operating out of excellence all the time I had been in his class, and that I was telling the truth. My mind was a blank and I was willing to take the F, because that's what I deserved. But I didn't have to.

I then realized that there are people out there who will give you a break once in a while. It was empowering. It was like he was saying, "I know who you are, not just what you do." That's an amazing gift to give somebody. I will be grateful to that guy till the day I die. I thought, "That's the kind of teacher I want to be."[26]

What an excellent example of how God has given us, undeserving sinners, salvation and immediate acceptance by Him through what his Son did on the cross for us. We are saved through faith in Jesus. This faith involves knowledge of the gospel (Romans 10:14), acknowledgment of the truth of its message, and personal reception of the Savior (John 1:12). Paul states that works cannot save (Ephesians 2:9), but that good works should always accompany salvation (James 2:17).

Even though we cannot make a complete biblical comparison from a story such as today's, we do find a teacher who bestowed grace on his pupil.

By all rights the student deserved an F on his grade, but the teacher was willing to give him an A because of who he was. The teacher knew the pupil's heart and his efforts of the past.

This is where we are in life without Christ. We deserve an F grade because we, in ourselves, are sinners and do not deserve anything more. However, Jesus went to the cross for us and died for our sins, so that by faith we would accept His act for us personally. Through God's grace, and His grace alone, and His grace only, our grade went from an F to an A because of our faith in God's Son, Jesus. The cross of Christ divides every other religion from Christianity. That's why the events surrounding the cross are paramount to us as Christians.

Father God, I come to You humbly in prayer, thanking You for Your grace upon my life. I would not want to go around for the rest of my life with an F stamped on me. There would be no hope in this world. Maybe that's why I see so many sad people. They have never received Your grace and have never gone from darkness to light. Thank You, thank You for my salvation through Your undeserved grace to me! Amen.

Taking Action

- Thank God for your salvation.
- If you haven't received the act of His grace, you might want to go through these verses of Scripture:

  Romans 3:23

  Romans 6:23

  Acts 16:30,31

  Ephesians 2:8,9

  Romans 10:9,10

  Luke 18:13

After reading these verses, you may want to invite Jesus Christ into your heart. If you do, you can pray this prayer:

Lord Jesus, I need You. Thank You for dying on the cross for my sins. I open the door of my life and receive You as my Savior and Lord. Thank You for forgiving my sins and giving me eternal life. Take control of the throne of my life. Make me the kind of person You want me to be.[27]

If you prayed this prayer, Christ will come into your life, as He promised.

Reading On

Revelation 3:20	Hebrews 13:5
1 John 5:11-13	Colossians 1:14

Grace is not sought, nor bought, nor wrought. It is a free gift of Almighty God to needy mankind.

— *Billy Graham*

Notes

1. Luci Swindoll, *Women's Devotional Bible* (Grand Rapids: Zondervan Corporation, 1960), p. 1375.
2. Erma Bombeck, further documentation unavailable.
3. Kay Arthur, taken from a newsletter dated March 1996, Precept Ministries, Chattanooga, TN.
4. Lee Roberts, *Praying God's Will for My Son* and *Praying God's Will for My Daughter* (Nashville: Thomas Nelson Publishers, 1993).
5. Donna Otto, *The Stay at Home Mom* (Eugene, OR: Harvest House Publishers, 1991), pp. 51-54.
6. Roberts, *Praying God's Will*.
7. Otto, *Stay at Home Mom*, pp. 51-54.
8. Rudyard Kipling, *Just So Stories*. This poem is the finale of "How the Camel Got Its Humps."
9. Elon Foster, ed., *Six Thousand Sermon Illustrations* (Grand Rapids: Baker Book House, 1992), p. 353.
10. Ann Landers, printed in the *Press Enterprise*, Riverside, CA, Saturday, May 11, 1996, p. B-10.
11. Steve Farrar, *Point Man* (Portland: Multnomah Books, a part of the Questar publishing family, 1990). Adapted from pp. 81-83.
12. Adapted from Temple Bailey. This story first appeared in a pamphlet that Clifton's Cafeteria distributed to its customers in 1945.
13. H. Norman Wright, *Communication: Key to Your Marriage* (Ventura, CA: Regal Books, 1974), p. 52.
14. Florence Littauer, *Silver Boxes, The Gift of Encouragement* (Waco, Texas: Word Publishing, 1989), pp. 1-4.
15. Harold L. Myra, *The Family Book of Christian Virtues*, edited by Stuart and Jill Briscoe (Colorado Springs: Alive Communications, Inc., 1995), p. 252.
16. Adapted from Foster, *Six Thousand Sermon Illustrations*, p. 627.
17. Dennis and Barbara Rainey, *Building Your Mate's Self-Esteem* (San Bernardino: Here's Life Publishers, 1986), p. 154.
18. *The Woman's Study Bible*, edited by Dorothy Kelley Patterson and Rhonda Harringon Kelley (Nashville: Thomas Nelson Publishers, 1995), p. 450.
19. Ibid., p. 2071.
20. Anne Ortlund, *Disciplines of the Beautiful Woman* (Waco, TX: Word, 1977), p. 29.

21. Dennis and Barbara Rainey, *Building Your Mate's Self-Esteem* (San Bernardino: Here's Life Publishers, 1986), pp. 56-57.

22. Michael Johnson, "If Talking the Talk, Walk the Walk," in *The Richmond Register*, June 21, 1996, Section B-1.

23. Steve Farrar, *Standing Tall* (Sisters, OR: Multnomah Books, 1994), pp. 51-52.

24. Charles R. Swindoll, *You and Your Child* (Nashville: Thomas Nelson Publishers, 1977), p. 64.

25. Paul Brandt and Philip Yancey, *In His Image* (Grand Rapids: Zondervan Publishing House, 1994), pp. 25-29.

26. Jane Bluestein, (Deerfield Beach, FL: Health Communications, Inc., 1995), pp. 12-13.

27. Bill Bright, *Four Spiritual Laws* (San Bernardino: Campus Crusade for Christ Inc., 1965), p. 10.

For more information regarding speaking engagements and additional material, please send a self-addressed stamped envelope to:

More Hours in My Day
2150 Whitestone Drive
Riverside, CA 92506

Other Harvest House Books
by Bob & Emilie Barnes

🍂 🍂 🍂

Books by
Bob & Emilie Barnes

*Minute Meditations
for Couples*

*A Little Book of Manners
for Boys*

Abundance of the Heart

*15 Minute Devotions
for Couples*

Books by Emilie Barnes

The 15-Minute Organizer

15 Minutes Alone with God

*15 Minutes of Peace
with God*

101 Ways to Lift Your Spirits

*The Busy Woman's Guide
to Healthy Eating*

A Tea to Comfort Your Soul

A Cup of God's Love

A Cup of Hope

A Different Kind of Miracle

*Emilie's Creative
Home Organizer*

*Everything I Know
I Learned from My Garden*

Fill My Cup, Lord

Friends Are a Blessing

Friends of the Heart

Help Me Trust You, Lord

If Teacups Could Talk

An Invitation to Tea

Join Me for Tea

*Keep It Simple
for Busy Women*

Let's Have a Tea Party!

A Little Book of Manners

*Minute Meditations
for Busy Moms*

*Minute Meditations
for Women*

More Hours in My Day

The Promise of Hope

Safe in the Father's Hands

*Strength for Today,
Bright Hope for Tomorrow*

Survival for Busy Women

The Twelve Teas of Christmas

*The Twelve Teas
of Friendship*

Books by Bob Barnes

*15 Minutes Alone with God
for Men*

Minute Meditations for Men

*What Makes a Man
Feel Loved*